UNDERSTA
COMPANY
ACCOUNTS

The Daily Telegraph
ESSENTIAL MANAGEMENT TECHNIQUES

UNDERSTANDING COMPANY ACCOUNTS

BOB ROTHENBERG & JOHN NEWMAN
BLICK ROTHENBERG & NOBLE

Published by Telegraph Publications,
Peterborough Court, At South Quay,
181 Marsh Wall, London E14 9SR

Series Editor: Marlene Garsia

Typeset by Bookworm Typesetting, Manchester

Printed in Great Britain by Biddles Ltd, Guildford

British Library Cataloguing in Publication Data

Rothenberg, Bob
Understanding company accounts.——(Essential management techniques).
1. Corporations——Accounting 2. Financial statements
I. Title II. Series
657′.95 HF5686.C7

ISBN 0–86367–191–8

Contents

Foreword and Acknowledgements

We have tried to avoid getting tied up in technicalities in this book, and consequently some of our accountant friends might take issue with points of detail, for if anything we have erred on the side of simplicity.

The accounts of the Infallible group do not always live up to their name! Our aim is that, overall, the book should give a true and fair view of accounts and their meaning. It takes account of legislation as at 31 October 1987.

We should like to express our thanks to David Rothenberg MA, FCA, of Blick Rothenberg & Noble, and to Pippa Rothenberg, each of whom read the typescript and made invaluable comments; to our editor Marlene Garsia of William Curtis Limited for her expert guidance; and to Carole Anderson for her unflagging hard work in typing the book. Such faults as remain are all our own.

Bob Rothenberg and John Newman,
London 1987.

Introduction

This book is not written for accountants. It is not even written for aspiring accountants. It is written for businessmen, the kind of people for whom accountants produce their reports. It will not teach you how to prepare accounts, for as most accountants will tell you it took them long, tedious months of study and practice before they came to grips with their profession. Fortunately, though, you do not have to be able to play a piano to recognise a good tune.

Our intention is that having read this book you should be able to discover whether the message from a set of accounts is good or bad. You should also be able to judge how well the management of the business is performing. We also explain the meaning of the jargon used by professional accountants. But apart from what is necessary for understanding this language, we will keep the use of 'accountant-speak' to a minimum.

Double-Entry Accounting

All accounts are prepared on the basis of a system of double-entry book-keeping or accounting, a system which has successfully operated for several hundred years. Although we are not going to teach you double-entry book-keeping, some familiarity with the term will be useful. It is not, however, necessary to learn double-entry book-keeping to understand accounts.

The essence of double-entry book-keeping is that two entries are made for every transaction.

Example

You buy a word processor for £500, and pay cash for it. Your accountant or book-keeper makes two entries in your books. First, he adds £500 to your business assets, representing the amount paid by your business for the word processor now owned by it. Second, he reduces your cash balance by £500, the amount of cash spent in acquiring the asset.

Similarly, two entries will be made for each and every other financial transaction carried out by the business. One entry will be called a debit (in our case the asset – the word processor – now owned by the business). The other entry will be called a credit (in our case the reduction in the cash balance). The total value of debits should always equal the total value of credits. Your accountant can then inform you that the books balance. If the books do not balance this will indicate that an error has been made in recording a transaction somewhere along the line.

Some 10 or 20 years ago, accountants spent many hours a month balancing the books, tracking down and correcting errors made earlier in the month. Today, despite the widespread use of computers in keeping accounting records, accountants still continue to spend many hours a month balancing the books. (The term books is still used even when the records are computer-based.) However, the fact that the books balance merely means that the arithmetic is right; it does not mean that the business results are good.

What Are Accounts?

The accounting records, or books, list in detail all of the company's financial transactions during a given period of time. Accounts summarise the transactions recorded in the books during that period and show you the position at the end of it. The period covered by published accounts is normally one year. Unpublished internal accounts can cover any period. Monthly accounts are quite common.

The essentials of a set of accounts are two documents: a *profit and loss account* and a *balance sheet*. Imagine you are presented with the accounts of a business for the calendar year 1986. The profit and loss account covers the entire year and will show you what the sales of the business were and what its expenses were during that period. The difference between the two will be the profit or loss the business made in the course of the year. This will be added, after deducting any tax payable to the government and any dividends payable to the owners of the business, to the balance sheet.

The balance sheet will show you how the business stands at the end of the year: the cost of business assets (less any amounts written off that cost), sums of money owed to the business, sums of money which the business owes to third parties and, finally, the amount which, in a sense, it owes to its owners – the sums of money which they originally contributed to the business as the business capital, plus the profits after tax subsequently earned by the business not paid out to the owners. The balance sheet is a snapshot of the position at the close of business on the last day of the year. There is a lot more to it than that, of course. We will consider profit and loss accounts and balance sheets in rather more detail in later chapters of this book.

When talking about a business's profits, many businessmen make the mistake of using the term balance sheet when what they really mean is profit and loss account. They talk about the profit for the year shown by the balance sheet when, as we have seen, the *annual* profit is actually shown by the profit and loss account. This is a real give away to accountants. Do not make that mistake. The confusion is probably caused because the balance sheet includes *total* profits to date not paid out to the owners.

A third document usually found in sets of accounts is a cash flow statement, sometimes called a *statement of source and application of funds*. This shows the ways in which cash flows into the business, the ways it is spent and the amount left over.

A set of accounts will also include a greater or lesser number of notes and back-up schedules setting out more details of items contained in the basic documents.

Company and Group Accounts

Often a business is run as a limited liability company, a separate legal entity which the law treats as a person in its own right. Most legislation concerning companies is now contained in the Companies Act 1985.

Most company accounts are prepared for a single company, a single business entity. However, many businesses are organised these days as groups of interlocking companies, one of which is the master company which owns or controls all of the others. A group of companies might be organised in such a way that one company, call it Infallible Limited, owns 100 per cent of two other companies, Bertie Limited and Cecil Limited, with Bertie Limited in turn owning 75 per cent of Dellboy Limited. Thus, the company structure resembles building blocks as shown in Figure 1.1 below.

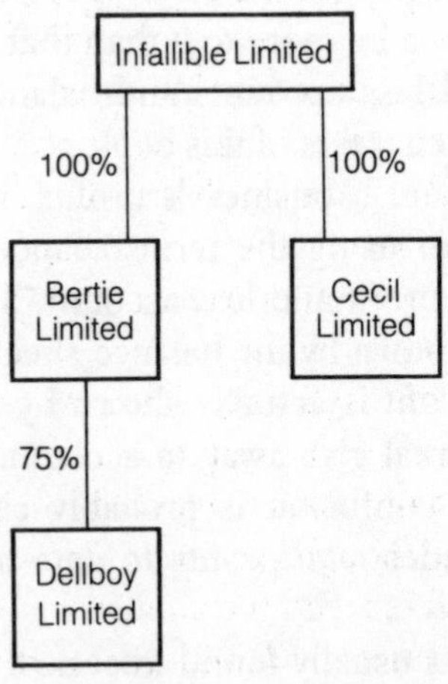

Figure 1.1 Company Ownership Structure

Each company will prepare its own accounts, but Infallible Limited, in addition to preparing its own accounts, will also prepare group accounts for the group as a whole. Group accounts will disclose the total results and total net assets of all the companies owned or controlled by Infallible Limited in proportion to its ownership of them. We will use examples taken from the accounts of the Infallible group throughout this book (see Appendix on page 168).

Unincorporated Businesses

Not all businesses are organised as companies. Many small businesses are carried on by one individual or by two or more trading as partners. There is no necessity for the name of the business to consist of the names of the individuals concerned.

Such businesses need accounts too but their accounts are not regulated by the Companies Act, do not have to be audited, and are not placed anywhere on public record. In other respects, however, they will be put to the same uses as company accounts. They will be used internally by management and both the Inland Revenue and the businesses' bankers will want to see them.

A Word of Caution

Balancing the books is not the be-all and end-all of accountancy. Certainly, the books have to balance. If they do not balance then something is very definitely wrong. Unfortunately, though, the reverse is not also true. The fact that the books balance does not mean that everything is correct, not even when the books balance to the penny.

If your accountant tells you that the books balance so everything must be all right, maintain an element of scepticism. There are a number of things that could still be wrong.

Suppose you had bought the word processor for £500 but your accountant had entered the sum in the books as £600. If he increased business assets by £600, what he thought was the cost of the word processor, and also reduced the cash balance by £600, the books would still balance since the same sum would have been entered on both sides. But they would be wrong. Business assets would be overstated by £100 and the cash balance would be understated by this sum. The error would be discovered when the cash balance was counted and found to be £100 more than was recorded in the books. If he then went back and checked each entry in the books which related to cash, he would eventually find that the invoice for the word processor was for £500 whereas the entry in the books was for £600. The entry could then be corrected. But can you imagine how much more difficult the task would be if the invoice for the purchase of the word processor had not been retained?

Taking another example, suppose that your accountant completely forgot to enter the word processor transaction. In such a case, business assets would be understated by £500, representing the cost of the word processor, which the business actually owns, but the cash balance would be overstated by £500, since the sum of £500 which had been spent would not have been recorded. Again, the books would still balance. The error would only be discovered when someone counted the cash. He would find £500 less in the cash box than would be recorded in the books. Everyone would know that something was wrong, but unless they could locate the lost invoice there would be little that they could do to make the correction. They could, of course, check all the business assets and then find that there was not a word processor recorded in the books, but they would still have to go one step further to find out when the word processor was bought and how much it actually cost.

Such errors are known as errors of omission, and can be particularly difficult to make good. This is why, when a businessman scans a set of accounts, he should not just look to see what is there: he should also look to see what is not there.

Inherent Uncertainty in Accounts

Both of these errors are at least capable of being corrected to make the accounts 100 per cent right. There is a third possibility, however. Going back to our example, everybody knows that a word processor will last for more than one year. Everyone also knows that it will not last forever. It would seem reasonable to charge its cost against profits over each of the years in which it will be used. This is done by charging it as an expense (known as depreciation) in the profit and loss account over the period of its life, and therefore over several accounting years.

Unfortunately, no-one knows exactly how long the word

processor will last or what its second-hand value will be, if anything, at the end of its life. It may last five years and then be thrown on the junk heap. We would therefore write off its cost of £500 over five years at £100 per year. Someone else might think that it would last 10 years and still have a second-hand value of £50 at the end of that period. Such a person might write it off over 10 years at £45 per year (£500−£50 = £450 ÷ 10). Who would be right? Maybe neither, and no-one will know until the word processor is finally scrapped or sold. In the meantime, there is an unavoidable element of uncertainty.

This may seem like a trivial example, and it is. But there are usually anything from a dozen to a hundred or more elements of uncertainty in every set of accounts you see. The number depends on the complexity of the accounts, and not all of these are so trivial. Some can involve very large figures indeed.

What conclusions can we draw? That accounts are not worth the paper they are printed on? A tempting answer, perhaps, but that would be going too far. The fact that it is not possible to arrive at 100 per cent certainty in a set of accounts is no excuse for not trying to get as near to that figure as one can. After all, the reason that we need accounts is because we want to get the best estimate of what is actually going on. We want to get as close to the truth as we possibly can. So do not worry unduly about every last pound, accept that there is an element of uncertainty, and understand that some, but not all, of the figures in a set of accounts will be approximate. By the time you reach the end of this book you will understand what to look out for and what to look upon with scepticism. You will have a feeling for how to use accounts for your company's benefit.

1

Published Accounts

Accounts may be divided into two broad categories. First there are published accounts which are available to, and may be used by, people outside a business. Second there are internal accounts which are used by the managers of a business, the circulation of which is strictly restricted. This chapter will consider published accounts; the next chapter will look at internal accounts.

Requirement to Publish Accounts

The directors of a limited company are required by the Companies Act to produce and publish annual financial statements for that company, commonly known as accounts. These will normally cover a period of 12 months and must be drawn up each year to the same month end. A company's financial year (its accounting year) does not necessarily have to be the calendar year, although 31 December remains the most popular year end. Companies are permitted to change their accounting year end occasionally, although the number of times that they may do so is limited. In no case can accounts cover a period which is less than 6 months or more than 18 months. All published accounts also have to show the figures reported in the previous set of accounts for comparison.

Over the past 100 years rules and conventions have been introduced in order to make one company's published accounts appear similar in format and style to another. In the course of this book we will provide an explanation of the current format of published accounts.

One important concept has emerged which now underlies all published accounts. This is that they must show what is called a *true and fair* view of the company's profit or loss for the period and of its financial position at the end of the period.

True and fair

The term true and fair has evolved comparatively recently. It was first written into company law by the Companies Act of 1948. Before that, company law required accounts to be true and correct, and earlier still other phrases were used. The 1948 Act did not define the term true and fair. Even now no legal definition of the phrase is available, so what exactly does it mean?

We suggest that accounts should be true in that:

(a) They should be in accordance with all the known facts.

(b) Figures which are capable of correct and precise measurement within the time scale available should be so measured.

We would suggest that accounts should be fair in that:

(a) Those figures which are surrounded by inherent uncertainties and cannot by their nature be 100 per cent correct should be honest.

(b) The view given by the accounts should not be misleading.

(c) The accounts should be straightforward and reasonable.

Overall, a reader should get a balanced impression of the business from the accounts.

In addition to being true and fair, there is a legal requirement for published accounts to be presented in a standard format, which is strictly regulated. Certain financial details, prescribed by the Companies Act, are required to be disclosed. Two directors have to sign the accounts to show that they have been approved by the board of directors as a whole.

Once the directors have completed the accounts there is a statutory obligation for an independent firm of auditors to report on the truth and fairness of the accounts and on whether they comply with the Companies Act. The significance of audit reports is discussed in Chapter 12.

The London Stock Exchange imposes certain additional requirements on quoted companies. These are required to send annual audited accounts to shareholders within six months of the end of the accounting period; most send them within four months or so. They are also required to show additional information in annual accounts, such as earnings per share. The shareholders must also be sent simplified half-yearly accounts.

Directors' report

In addition to the detailed figures and notes contained in the audited accounts, an accompanying directors' report also has to be published. This report is not audited, but if what it says is inconsistent with the accounts themselves the auditors have to say so. The directors' report has to include comparatively subjective items, such as a review by the directors of the development of the business during the year, details of important events which have happened after the accounting period, and what the directors see as likely future developments in the business.

Quoted companies, and some others, also include a chairman's report which expands on the same topics. We discuss directors' reports and chairman's reports in Chapter 11.

Public and private companies

A public company is a limited liability company which states in its Memorandum of Association (its basic constitution) that it is a public company. It must have a minimum allotted share capital of £50,000, at least 25 per cent of which must be paid up. It must also have complied with certain other not very onerous procedures which are laid down in the Companies Act. Any company which does not meet these conditions is a private company.

A public company is allowed to offer its shares to the public; a private company is not permitted to so do and, because of this all quoted companies have to be public companies. However, the common misconception that all public companies are quoted companies is just that – a misconception; many public companies are unquoted and privately owned.

Public companies will have the letters plc (standing for public limited company) at the end of their names. The letters may be written in capital letters and possibly with full stops. Private companies will have the word Limited (often abbreviated to Ltd) as the last word of their name.

Some businesses trade with a name that ends with neither plc nor Ltd, nor any allowable alternative to these. You should look at documentation issued by that business to see who the owner is; an invoice or brochure should yield this information. You will then be able to see whether it is an individual, a partnership, a plc or a Ltd.

Where and how to find published accounts

The audited accounts of private companies are required by law to be laid before a general meeting of shareholders of the company within 10 months of the end of the accounting period which they cover. In the case of public companies this period is reduced to 7 months. For companies with overseas interests these periods are extended by 3 months.

As well as being distributed to shareholders, the accounts of companies also have to be placed on public record. This is known as *filing* the accounts and is done, for English and Welsh companies, at Companies Registration Office in Cardiff. Copies of what is on record at Cardiff are kept at Companies House in London. In the case of Scottish companies, the accounts have to be filed in Edinburgh. In the case of companies registered in Northern Ireland, which are regulated by a separate Companies Act, the accounts have to be filed in Belfast.

Any member of the public may inspect these records and obtain a microfiche copy of what is on file. There are a number of specialised agencies which will carry out a company search on your behalf. Their fees range from about £10 upwards, depending on the information you require.

Modified accounts

Small and medium-sized private companies are permitted to file what are known as modified accounts on public record with the Registrar of Companies. However, they still have to send normal non-modified accounts to their shareholders. If they wish to file modified accounts they have to produce two separate sets of accounts and incur more expense than they otherwise would.

Small companies

Modified accounts for small companies consist only of a basic balance sheet, the amount of detail on which is very much restricted, and a few other items of information. Neither a profit and loss account nor a directors' report has to be included.

Essentially, a small company is one which can meet at least two of the following three conditions:

1. Sales of not more than £2 million.
2. Total assets before deducting liabilities of not more than £975,000.
3. No more than 50 employees.

Medium-sized companies

As far as medium-sized companies are concerned, modified accounts merely restrict the amount of information shown on the profit and loss account. Other than that, all other details required in normal non-modified accounts have to be included. In order to qualify as medium-sized, a company has to satisfy at least two of the following three conditions:

1. Sales of not more than £8 million.
2. Total assets before deducting liabilities of not more than £3,900,000.
3. No more than 250 employees.

People sometimes think that if modified accounts are filed the companies concerned might have something to hide. Sometimes, modified accounts are filed to protect information that the company feels will be of advantage to its competitors; in other cases they are filed because the directors believe that the less that is available on public record the better. But whichever the reason, caution should be exercised; the information that will be available to a non-shareholder could be substantially less than that available for other companies.

The accounts of the Infallible group, which are discussed in this book, are not modified accounts, although the group would qualify as a medium-sized group.

Group Accounts

As mentioned in the Introduction, a company which owns or controls other companies is required to publish accounts for the group as a whole. Such accounts will normally be headed *consolidated accounts*: there will be a consolidated profit and loss account, a consolidated balance sheet and a consolidated statement of source and application of funds.

Consolidated accounts combine the information to be found in the individual profit and loss accounts, balance sheets and statements of source and application of funds of each company in the group. They show the overall position for the group as a whole. If group companies are not owned 100 per cent by the parent company (either directly or indirectly) the proportion of the year's profit which is not 'owned' by the parent company will be eliminated from the consolidated profit and loss account, and described as *minority interests*.

The total combined assets of each company in the group will be shown in the consolidated balance sheet. The proportion of the group's assets attributable to shareholders outside the parent company will be shown as *minority interests* in the consolidated balance sheet. The accounting entries which have to be made to achieve this result are highly technical and complex.

In addition to the consolidated balance sheet, the individual balance sheet of the parent company will also be published with the group accounts. Companies which publish group accounts are not, however, required to publish their own individual profit and loss accounts, or statements of source and application of funds.

So what is a group of companies? A group of companies is simply a parent company and all its subsidiaries. A company is a subsidiary if the parent company owns more than 50 per cent of its voting equity share capital, or if it owns at least one share in it and controls the composition of its board of directors. In addition, a company is a subsidiary of the parent if it is a subsidiary of another company which is itself a subsidiary of the parent. In company law, a parent company is termed a *holding company*.

Virtually every quoted company is a parent company, so virtually all the accounts published by quoted companies are consolidated accounts. Each individual subsidiary company still has to publish its own accounts in the same way as any independent company.

Group accounts must show the name of all subsidiary companies, together with the proportion of the share capital of each which is owned. For principal subsidiaries, they also have to disclose the nature of their business.

The accounts of all subsidiary companies have to disclose the name of their ultimate holding company. The *ultimate holding company* is the parent company at the top of the pyramid of group companies. In Figure 1.1 (page 13) Infallible Limited would be Dellboy Limited's ultimate holding company, although Bertie Limited would be its immediate holding company.

Associated companies

Group accounts may also include the results of *associated companies*. A company is an associated company if the group owns less than 50 per cent of its shares, but owns enough on a long-term basis to exercise a significant influence over the company. A shareholding of 20 per cent or more of the equity voting rights is normally thought to be sufficient to give such influence. Partners in a joint venture or consortium company will also see that company as an associated company.

The term associated company is used by an accounting standard; in company law the term *related company* is used. Although the definitions are technically not identical they can be treated as being the same for most practical purposes.

The group's consolidated profit and loss account will include, separately identified, its share of the profits of all associated companies for the year. However, the assets of the associated companies are not taken up in the consolidated balance sheet. The names of associated companies have to be disclosed in the notes to the accounts.

Accounting Standards

Published accounts are drawn up using the generally accepted accounting principles and conventions of the day. Some of these have been codified by the Accounting Standards Committee in the British Isles into statements of standard accounting practice. These may be referred to by some people as SSAPs. Many of the statements cover those areas of accounts where accounting practices might otherwise diverge between different companies. Where accounts do not comply with accounting standards they should say why not, and what the effect is.

Accounting standards have played their part in improving what might be called the truth and fairness of published accounts, but they have not been an unqualified success. Many grey areas remain, and some of the standards themselves permit alternative treatments of similar items in different reporting companies.

There are also international accounting standards, but, to be honest, these have little impact on most businesses in the UK, where standards are consistent with those abroad.

Fundamental accounting concepts

The most important of the accounting standards identifies four fundamental accounting concepts. These underlie all published accounts. Their use is not highlighted in the accounts of any particular company or group because these fundamental accounting concepts have such general acceptance. It should be assumed that they have been followed unless something to the contrary is said.

The first of these is the *consistency* concept. This says no more than that like items should be treated consistently from one accounting period to the next, which is only normal common sense. The other three concepts are the *prudence* concept, the *accruals* concept and the *going concern* concept. We will introduce them at appropriate points in the book.

Accounting policies

Another particularly significant area of accounting standards is that they require companies and groups to disclose their principal accounting policies. In non-accountant's language, *accounting policies* are the methods used by a business to account for transactions where more than one possible method is available. They will be set out either as the first note to the accounts or on a separate page of their own. It is important to watch out for unusual accounting policies when reviewing other company's accounts, since such policies can significantly affect the figures shown in the accounts and therefore the impression given by the accounts.

Typically, accounting policies may, inter alia, cover:

1. The basis of consolidation and the basis of accounting for associated companies (see this chapter and Chapter 5).
2. Depreciation basis and rates (see Chapter 5).
3. Deferred taxation (see Chapters 4 and 8).
4. Valuation of stocks and work in progress (see Chapter 6).
5. Treatment of transactions in foreign currency (see Chapters 6 and 7).
6. Basis of accounting for goodwill (see Chapter 5).
7. Basis of turnover figure (see Chapter 3).
8. Leasing transactions (see Chapter 10).
9. Pension scheme arrangements (see Chapter 7).
10. Treatment of research and development (see Chapter 5).

In addition, they will state whether the accounts have been prepared on the normal *historical cost* basis or on a *current cost* basis. The former simply means that assets and expenses are recorded in the accounts at what they originally cost. Most accounts are prepared substantially on the historical cost basis but with the inclusion of land and buildings at a valuation. This is the normal commonsense basis. The alternative method of preparing accounts is on a current cost basis. Accounts prepared on this basis are often known as CCA accounts.

CCA accounts

Current cost accounts have two aims. The main one is to ensure that a company does not report profits unless it has first maintained the physical resources of its business by ensuring that it has sufficient resources to replace all the assets which have been consumed in the year. Let us explain. In a time of inflation, a profit is easily made by buying stock at one price, waiting for a price rise and then selling at the higher price. However, unless a business makes profits over and above the inflation rate, it might not subsequently have sufficient financial resources to buy an equivalent quantity of new stock to replace the stock it has sold. This would be because the cost of buying new stock had risen. Similar considerations apply to replacing worn out plant and machinery.

The second aim of current cost accounting is to record assets in the balance sheet at their value to the business.

The first aim of current cost accounting is achieved by charging costs to the profit and loss account, not on the basis of the historical costs actually incurred, but on the basis of the cost of replacing the resources used. The second aim is achieved by recording assets in the balance sheet at what it would cost to replace them in their present condition.

There used to be an accounting standard requiring large companies to produce accounts on a current cost basis. Such accounts were in addition to accounts produced on the traditional historical cost basis and were usually referred to as supplementary current cost accounts. The accounting standard was suspended in June 1985 – some would say abandoned – as more and more large companies chose not to comply with it. In view of this, we will not deal further with the subject in this book.

Banking, insurance and shipping companies

Many banking, insurance and shipping companies are exempt from many of the rules and disclosure requirements applicable to other companies. They are, however, subject to other requirements. These special cases are outside the scope of this book.

2

Internal Accounts

Accounts which are published, sent to shareholders and made available to the general public will be true and fair and will comply with all the requirements applicable to them. They will, however, rarely give information over and above the minimum required, although there is nothing to prevent them from so doing. Taking into account all the supporting notes, the balance sheet will be fairly comprehensive. However, the profit and loss account will be less so. The amount of detail will be very limited. Amongst accountants, the published profit and loss account is often referred to as the *statutory profit and loss account* since its published form arises solely from statutory requirements.

For internal use, many companies will often attach a more comprehensive profit and loss account, known as a *detailed profit and loss account*, to the back of the accounts, inserting a note in front of it which says something to the effect that 'the pages which follow are only for the information of the directors and do not form part of the statutory accounts'. The detailed profit and loss account will also be sent to the Inspector of Taxes and to banks along with the statutory accounts. Those details contained in it which do not appear in the statutory profit and loss account are not audited.

However, these detailed profit and loss accounts are hardly sufficient to enable management to run the business on a day-to-day basis. For this they will need more regular and more detailed internal accounts produced with their specific needs in mind. Internal accounts do not have to be audited and do not, by their nature, have to comply with any legislative requirements. Internal accounts are usually referred to as *management accounts*, which means that they are produced for the purpose of assisting management in doing its job.

Management Accounts and Financial Accounts

The distinction between management and financial accounts is much loved by management accountants. Management accountants will be eager to explain that financial accountancy is merely a sub-division of management accountancy. Management accounting embraces the entire spectrum of accountancy they will say; financial accounting is largely about score-keeping. So what are the differences, and how real are they?

In their purest form financial accounts are merely descriptive. They will describe each item of expenditure in the profit and loss account by its nature, and aggregate all similar items of expenditure together on a global basis. All wages expenditure will be put together under the single category of wages. All rent paid will be aggregated together as one figure. Management accounts will provide a more detailed breakdown of individual items of income and expenditure. Wages could be broken down by function. Rent could be charged to different departments.

The manager's job is sometimes defined as planning, decision-making and controlling. The detail of management accounts should be designed to provide the manager with information to help him carry out each of these tasks. It is up to him to decide what information he needs as a basis for planning, making decisions and for controlling the implementation of those decisions, although it is always open to his accountant to make suggestions. Management accounts can therefore look very different in different industries, or between different businesses in the same industry. Management accounts are there to serve management teams and their particular needs.

Before looking at a set of accounts a manager should ask himself a few questions. 'What matters am I going to decide, if any, on the basis of reading these accounts? What information do I therefore need, by when do I need it, and how precise does it have to be, to assist me in making those decisions? What information will I subsequently need to enable me to monitor the implementation of those decisions? What information do I need to be able to monitor the implementation of decisions taken in the past?'

The manager should then decide which area of the accounts he is going to give his attention to, and, if he is in the happy position of being able to obtain it, what additional one-off information he might need. It is otherwise easy to get lost in a mass of figures or to waste time on aspects of accounts which are irrelevant to one's real needs.

Consider the case of a manager, looking at the management accounts of his business, who may be faced with an overwhelming profusion of figures. Usually, the same categories of information will be churned out month after month.

At different times though he may be considering quite different aspects of the business. In April the manager may find his mind concentrated on cash flow. In September he may be carrying out a review of margins, overheads and profitability. In November he may be thinking about the results which his company will report to shareholders in the annual financial accounts to the end of December, and about whether he should be taking any last minute actions in the last month of the financial year.

The manager will concentrate on different areas of the accounts in each of these cases. Much of the detail will not be relevant to his immediate needs and can be skimmed through. Yet, in the particular areas which are of real concern, additional detailed information may be called for.

Key points

There is a great deal of truth in the saying that the key points, the points relevant to immediate decision-taking needs or the key figures which put all the other figures in perspective, can be written on a single page. Try to get your company accountant to do this for you. Also ask him to summarise other salient features of the accounts and to highlight any significant or unusual points. Such a practice will also re-inforce and strengthen the company accountant's sense of involvement as part of the team.

It should also reduce the likelihood of any significant points being missed.

Costs

There are a number of different ways in which costs can be categorised in management accounts, other than simply listing them out by their nature as is done in financial accounts. Costs can be divided between fixed costs and variable costs. They can also be collected in cost centres or apportioned to cost units.

Fixed and variable costs

Variable costs are sometimes called *direct costs* or *prime costs*. They are the costs which are specifically or directly related to the end product produced by the business. In a manufacturing business they will vary with the volume of output. The three components of variable costs are *labour*, *materials* and *expenses*. Labour consists of the wages and salaries of those people directly producing the end product. Materials comprise those items actually used to make the end product. Expenses might include items such as bought-in services, contract labour and equipment hire.

Fixed costs are sometimes called *indirect costs* or *overheads*. They are costs which are not specifically related to an end product and do not vary with the volume of output. They have two components, labour and expenses. On this occasion, labour comprises the wages and salaries of managers, supervisors, administrative staff and so on. Expenses are other items such as rent, rates, light, heat and insurance. Fixed costs can also include material costs, but these are usually fairly insignificant.

Variable costs and fixed costs are fairly easy to understand as descriptive items, but it is important to remember that the descriptions are not written in stone. Variable costs are fixed in the short term; labour, for instance, cannot be shed or taken on all that quickly. Similarly, fixed costs are variable in the long term; for instance, a company could relocate to cheaper or to more expensive premises.

Cost centres

Expenditure can also be broken down from broad descriptive categories, such as salaries, rent, rates, power and lighting, into amounts attributable to different departments. Such departments could include distribution, marketing, accounts and general administration. They might be based at different locations. They would often be referred to as cost centres. The accounts of each cost centre would show all items of expenditure attributable to it. The manager in charge of that cost centre would then have information to enable him to make decisions and to monitor the implementation of those decisions so as to take corrective action where necessary. His superior would be able to see the costs attributable to that particular department.

Costs, are said to be *allocated* to cost centres when one particular cost clearly relates exclusively to one particular cost centre. The cost of the labour used exclusively in a particular department would be a case in point. Costs are said to be *apportioned* to cost centres when a particular cost partly relates to each of several different cost centres. The rent and rates for an entire building would be apportioned over all the different cost centres which occupied that building, usually on the basis of the square footage occupied.

Cost units

Such analyses are obviously useful up to a point, but many management accounts will take the process one stage further. Here the concept of cost units might be used. Forget the associations of the word cost for the moment and view cost units as units of output, different products or services sold by the business. If a business sells chairs, then each chair is a cost unit. All that is meant by this is that all the costs attributable to each chair can be collected together.

But the chair's cost could be broken down into more detailed cost units. The legs of the chair, for example, could be a cost unit, the upholstery could be another, the main frame of the chair could be a third. The breakdown would depend upon what was appropriate to the circumstances of the business.

All the costs collected in cost centres should be allocated or apportioned to cost units if this method of accounting is to be used as a way of controlling costs and as a basis for decision-taking.

Pricing Decisions

Management accounts can also be used to assist management to make pricing decisions. The way the business is run and the basis on which the management wish to take decisions will, or ought to, determine the way in which the management accounts are drawn up and presented.

Pricing may be carried out on a *marginal cost* basis. On this basis, only variable costs are taken into account and the price is set so as to maximise the *contribution* which sales make towards fixed cost. The contribution made is simply the difference between revenue from sales and the variable costs attributable to those sales. There will be a particular price at which contribution is maximised, depending upon how sensitive the volume of sales is to price changes.

The market could be segmented. Different prices could be charged for the same product to different segments of the market. Sometimes, the price may be set by a market leader and the business will have little choice but to accept what it can get.

In such a situation the management accounts should be drawn up in such a way as to separate out variable costs from fixed costs and highlight the contribution made towards those fixed costs.

Alternatively, pricing may be carried out on a cost-plus basis, which is sometimes called *full cost pricing*. In its purest form, every single cost in the business, including every fixed cost, is allocated or apportioned to the end products, the final cost units. A decision is then taken as to what profit is required, and the profit element is added on to give the price to be charged. The profit element might be calculated so as to give a certain return on capital employed at a given level of output. It might include a premium to take account of the very high quality of the product or service being sold.

Variances

A discussion of budgeting methods and the different bases on which budgets can be drawn up is beyond the scope of the book. However, once plans and budgets have been drawn up management accounts will make comparisons between budgeted figures and what has actually happened. Differences will be inevitable. Management accounts will seek to highlight those variances, at least in financial terms. The term variance is used to describe the difference between what was expected, the budgeted figure, and the actual figure.

Providing information to enable the manager to monitor such variances, and hence to exercise control and take corrective action where necessary, is one of the most important functions that management accounts can fulfil. How else is a manager to know whether a budget has been met?

If a manager can translate into financial terms the expected effect of a decision which he has taken, he can also use management accounts as a way of checking whether or not the decision has been properly implemented. Most decisions can be translated into financial terms with the help of an accountant.

Management accounts need to be timely so that corrective action can also be taken quickly. It is usually better to get a figure today which is 80 per cent accurate than to get one which is 95 per cent accurate but which only arrives the month after. Managers will want to monitor some figures on a weekly or even daily basis.

Divisional and Regional Accounts

In the same way that published accounts can cover individual companies and groups, internal accounts can also be produced for larger or smaller entities within the overall structure of a business.

It is conceivable that a company which is a member of a group could also be organised in divisions and regions.

In our example in Figure 1.1, Dellboy is 75 per cent owned by Bertie, which is 100 per cent owned by Infallible. Bertie might be organised into two divisions for management purposes. Dellboy might also be split into two divisions, one of which is in turn subdivided into two regions. The reporting structure would then look like Figure 2.1 below:

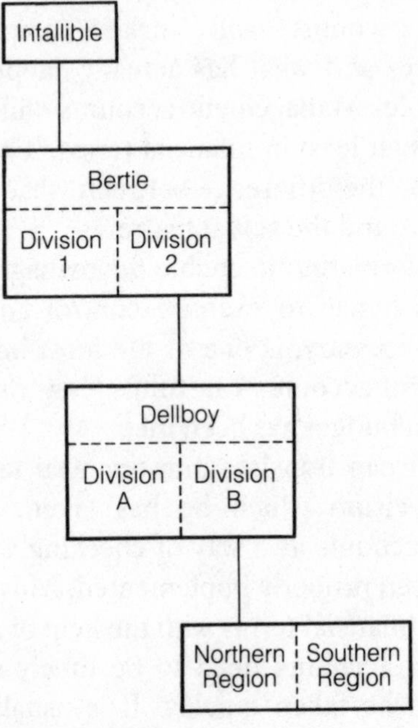

Figure 2.1

Management accounts should mirror this reporting structure. The manager in charge of Dellboy's Division B Southern Region would see the accounts for his region. The manager in charge of Dellboy's Division B as a whole would see management accounts for each individual region, together with the combined management accounts covering both regions.

If the two regions were really distinct then it would be important to ensure that losses made by one region were not masked by profit made by the other, as would happen if both were combined. Similarly, any truly distinct business unit or activity should have its own budget and management accounts to avoid this masking effect. By the same token, if the two regions were not really distinct, then it would be fairly pointless to treat them separately for management accounting purposes. It is important that management accounts should mirror the management structure of the business so that each manager can see the particular part of the business for which he is responsible.

Returning to our example, the manager of Dellboy Division B would also see the accounts for Division B as a whole (Division B might have divisional overheads which had not been apportioned to the regions). The manager in charge of Dellboy as a whole would see accounts for the entire company and so on.

If Dellboy Division B sold goods to Dellboy Division A, or to Bertie, or vice versa, then care has to be taken as to the price charged. It might well be group policy to buy goods from within the group wherever possible rather than from outside suppliers – this would almost always make sense for the group as a whole – but if prices charged to this captive market were too high or too low they would distort the relative profitabilities of the divisions or companies concerned. The same considerations with regard to *transfer pricing* arise when considering the published accounts of an individual company which is a member of a group. Its profit could have been distorted by the prices at which goods have been sold by one group company to another.

Internal Accounts and Published Audited Accounts

At the end of the financial year it will be necessary to reconcile the profit shown by unaudited, internal management accounts to the profit shown by the published audited accounts. Management should make sure that they understand the reason for each significant reconciling item.

Managers should accept that there will be differences between the figures in published accounts and figures in internal accounts. Partly this will be a question of time constraints. If internal accounts are to be produced quickly, and time is usually of the essence, then some accuracy will have to be sacrificed to timeliness. The more quickly the accounts are put together, the greater is the number of estimates which they contain and therefore the greater the scope for errors.

Partly, it will be a question of the two sets of accounts being produced on different bases. While published accounts are prepared on the historical cost basis, internal accounts might be prepared on a current cost basis. Depreciation will then be charged in published accounts based on a machine's original cost, but in internal accounts it will be based on the machine's estimated replacement price. This could be substantially higher, especially in times of high inflation.

Finally, elements of the internal accounts might plainly and simply be wrong. It does happen, so read the accounts very closely. If a figure is not what you think it should be or does not seem to make sense, then query it. Ask for a breakdown. Find out what business transactions the figure is supposed to represent. If the accounts do turn out to be incorrect then find out why the mistake occurred and what corrective action needs to be taken to ensure that it does not happen again. Any decisions taken on the basis of incorrect information should be reviewed.

Non-Financial Criteria

Although the information to be found in accounts is necessary in all areas of business you should not get *too* carried away. Financial criteria are not the *only* basis for decision taking, especially in the long term. A highly trained workforce and management team which is able to react quickly and successfully to unexpected events is also not without importance! Staff morale, corporate identity and brand image are almost always highly significant, but their achievement is difficult to measure in financial terms even though they will affect financial performance. The costs incurred in trying to achieve them can always be measured, however. Like all other costs, such costs need to be controlled, but achieving low costs in these areas as an objective in itself can be counter productive if by so doing the whole point of the expenditure is over ridden.

3

Profit and Loss Accounts – Pre-Tax Profits

We will first consider published profit and loss accounts, which will be laid out in a standard way. Then we will look at some of the ways in which management accounts might expand the information shown, or present the information in a different manner.

Published statutory profit and loss accounts must be laid out in one of two standard formats, called format 1 and format 2. This chapter will deal with pre-tax profits as shown in format 1 accounts. The next chapter will deal with post-tax profits and format 2 accounts. It will also illustrate a form of management accounts.

Accruals Concept

As a foreword, it should be emphasised that all profit and loss accounts – and, indeed, all accounts – are prepared in accordance with the underlying accounting principle called the accruals concept. This concept states that income and costs are accounted for in the period to which they relate, rather than the period in which they are received or paid. Accordingly, if a sale is made on credit terms, it is recorded as a sale when it is invoiced, not when the cash is received. Similarly, if a business receives an expense invoice, that invoice is accounted for on the basis of the date to which it relates, not the date when it is actually paid.

The accruals concept is sometimes called the *matching principle* since it also says that costs and revenues are always matched to each other. If they were not so matched then the true profit and loss made on any transaction would not be shown.

As discussed in Chapter 1, there is another underlying accounting principle called the *prudence concept*. This states that expenses, losses and liabilities are recognised at the earliest possible opportunity, whilst profits are not recognised until they can be seen in the form of cash or near cash. Where the accruals concept and the prudence concept conflict, the latter prevails. This reflects the basic conservatism with which published profit and loss accounts are produced.

The Infallible group's consolidated profit and loss account, which is produced under format 1, is set out in Table 3.1 below.

Table 3.1

Infallible Limited
Consolidated Profit and Loss Account
for the Year Ended 30 September 1987

	Note	*1987* £	*1986* £
Turnover	2	3,400,000	3,000,000
Cost of sales		1,200,000	1,150,000
Gross profit		2,200,000	1,850,000
Operating expenses	3	1,810,000	1,665,700
		390,000	184,300
Other income	4	6,400	5,700
		396,400	190,000
Interest payable and similar charges	5	23,400	11,000
Profit on ordinary activities before taxation	6	373,000	179,000
Tax on profit on ordinary activities	7	130,000	66,300
Profit on ordinary activities after taxation		243,000	112,700
Profit attributable to minority interests		1,000	700
Extraordinary item	8	40,000	–

Profit for the financial year	202,000	112,000
Retained profit at 1 October 1986	446,000	334,000
Retained profit at 30 September 1987	648,000	446,000

The same format is used both for profit and loss accounts of individual companies and for consolidated profit and loss accounts of groups. Apart from the first five lines it is not a particularly logical layout but it is the one the law requires. We will now look at each line in turn.

Turnover

The turnover of a company is the sales it makes to its customers for the provision of goods and services falling within its ordinary activities exclusive of VAT and trade discounts. If you are looking at the consolidated accounts of a group of companies then the turnover shown will be that for sales to customers outside the group. It is likely that some companies within the group will have sold goods and services to each other but such sales will have been eliminated from the consolidated accounts. The exact basis of arriving at turnover will be set out in one of the accounting policy notes.

The Infallible group's accounting policy is as follows: *turnover represents the invoiced value of goods sold, excluding sales between group companies, VAT and trade discounts.*

If a company or group has two or more substantially different classes of business then it is required to analyse its turnover between those different classes of business and to show this analysis as a note to the profit and loss account. It will also have to show the profit or loss before tax made by each of those classes of business.

Similarly, if a company supplied two different geographical markets then it will have to provide a further analysis of its turnover between those markets. Most companies interpret this requirement fairly broadly. Areas such as the UK, Europe,

North America, Asia, and the Rest of the World are widely used.

The Infallible group's analysis of turnover is set out in Table 3.2 below.

Table 3.2

Turnover

	1987	*1986*
	£	£
Geographical analysis		
UK	3,000,000	2,700,000
North America	400,000	300,000
	3,400,000	3,000,000

When you look at turnover, you will get your first indication of the size of the business. Is its turnover measured in millions of pounds, or tens of millions or hundreds of millions, or even more? Second, you will see the relative importance of the different classes of business undertaking, both in terms of size and of profitability, although in practice the directors may be pretty cagey about the sort of details which they disclose. Third, you will see where the customers reside. Whether having a high proportion of UK, European or North American customers is good, bad or unimportant is for you to decide. It will depend upon which markets you think are growing and which are in decline, how competitive you think conditions are in different markets and whether you think likely future exchange rate movements will be adverse or favourable to the company.

With a set of internal management accounts you could get much more precise figures if you wanted them. You could have turnover broken down in terms of individual salesmen or sales managers, if this information would help you to run the business. You might want sales to major customers to be separately identified. You might want a separate analysis of sales to new customers, or a statement of customers lost, giving the sales made to them in the previous period. Similarly, the number and value of credit notes issued could be analysed, giving the reasons for the credits. You ought to decide what information you want at the start of the year so that sales can be properly coded or analysed when the books are written up.

Just as important, or more important, than the absolute figures are the trends. Indeed, trends should be examined for each item in the accounts. For turnover, compare this year's sales with last year's figures, and with figures over the last four or five years. Is the business growing or contracting and does the trend vary between classes of the company's business or between the different geographical markets? Is growth or decline steady, or is it an up and down and unstable sort of business?

Reduce the absolute numbers in the accounts to percentages, which are usually easier to work with. Again, this is something which can be done for all items in the accounts. Look at what turnover was, say five years ago, and see by what percentage it has grown each year since then. There is no need to bother with decimal points, at least in the first instance; it is better to deliberately round each percentage to the nearest whole number. Studies have shown that round figures between 1 and 100 have much more meaning for most people than figures calculated to 5 or 6 decimal points.

If you are looking at management accounts then pinpoint fairly precisely where the variances in sales have arisen. Who is responsible for the class of business or the market concerned? Why has it happened? Has it happened because of changes in price or in volume? Are there external factors: is it price cutting by a competitor, competing products, an import embargo? Or is someone within the company not performing as he should? Are variances just temporary: what is the position on the current order bank? If the current order bank is very high, will additional funds be needed to finance the increased level of activity? We will look at the effect of changes in turnover on working capital in Chapter 7.

Operational gearing ratio

This ratio shows how sensitive net profits are to changes in turnover. The ratio is calculated as follows:

$$\frac{\text{turnover} - \text{variable costs}}{\text{trading profit}}$$

Variable costs are easily available from management accounts. In the case of published format 1 profit and loss accounts, variable costs could be taken as the items included in cost of sales and in distribution costs (see below) which are likely to vary with turnover.

Example

The Infallible group's turnover is £3.4 million, its costs of sales is £1.2 million, its distribution costs are £800,000 and trading profit on its ordinary activities before tax is £373,000. Its operational gearing would be 3.75, as calculated below:

$$\frac{3{,}400{,}000 - (1{,}200{,}000 + 800{,}000)}{373{,}000} = 3.75$$

This means that a 20 per cent increase in turnover would lead to a 75 per cent increase in trading profit (20 per cent x 3.75), as shown below:

	£	£
Turnover		
(£3,400,000 + 20%)		4,080,000
Cost of sales		
(£1,200,000 + 20%)	1,440,000	
Distribution costs		
(£800,000 + 20%)	960,000	

		2,400,000
		1,680,000
Administrative expenses	1,010,000	
Interest payable and similar charges	23,400	
Other income	(6,400)	1,027,000
Trading profit		653,000

The new trading profit of £653,000 is 75 per cent higher than the original trading profit of £373,000.

The comparable figure for the previous year was 6.2. In fact, the Infallible group has done rather better than might have been expected. It has increased its trading profit by 108 per cent on an increase in sales of 13 per cent. This is because it has made improvements in other areas (see below).

We have assumed that variable costs increase proportionately to turnover and that we have identified variable costs correctly. An element of scepticism may be justified on both counts. However, an increase in turnover of 20 per cent will clearly have very different results in a company with an operational gearing ratio of 3.75 compared with another company with a ratio of 1.75 and a third company with a ratio of 8.75.

Cost of Sales

This can be viewed as being the bulk of a company's variable costs including direct materials, direct labour and production overheads. Cost of sales will be arrived at after taking into account stocks still held at the end of the period and so will comprise the direct costs of those goods or services which have actually been sold. As with turnover, cost of sales, together with all other expenses in the profit and loss account, excludes VAT. Cost of sales is often not a very important figure in itself when compared to the next figure, gross profit.

Gross Profit

Gross profit is turnover less cost of sales. For managers within a company where the pricing decisions are made on a marginal cost method, the absolute size of this figure will be of overwhelming importance, at least in the short term.

For many people, though, in analysing the figures the absolute size of the figure will be less important than the *gross profit percentage*. The gross profit percentage is the gross profit expressed as a percentage of turnover.

Example

The Infallible group's turnover is £3,400,000, cost of sales is £1,200,000 and gross profit is £2,200,000. The gross profit percentage is 65 per cent calculated as follows:

$$\frac{2{,}200{,}000}{3{,}400{,}000} \times 100 = 65\%$$

Compare this year's gross profit percentage to last year's figure. Last year, the Infallible group's gross profit was 62 per cent. It has therefore increased its gross profit percentage by 3 per cent. Gross profit percentage should also be compared to the previous year to see if a trend is emerging. Is the company's gross profit percentage going up, declining or fluctuating? Do you know the norm for the industry, or the gross profit percentage made by the company's competitors?

When making such comparisons a word of caution is necessary. Not all companies play the game by exactly the same rules. Some will include items in cost of sales which others include lower down the profit and loss account under a heading such as administrative expenses. When the requirement to disclose gross profit was first introduced a few years ago, and the first sets of accounts published under the new rules became available, one well-known retail jewellery company found that the gross profit percentage which could be calculated from its accounts was double that of its competitors. Was it brilliantly profitable compared to its competitors? No. What had happened was that it had included expenses under the headings: distribution costs and administrative expenses, which its major competitors had all included under the heading cost of sales. Its final profit before tax, after all expenses had been charged, was broadly comparable to its competitors. With perhaps a little embarrassment the company concerned changed its method of allocating expenses between different expense headings in the published profit and loss account and fell into line.

In the retail trade, gross profit percentage is the corollary of mark-up. Gross profit percentage compares gross profit to turnover; mark-up compares gross profit to cost of sales.

Example

The Infallible group's gross profit is £2,200,000 and cost of sales is £1,200,000. The mark up is 183 per cent calculated as follows:

$$\frac{2,200,000}{1,200,000} \times 100 = 183\%$$

Where the gross profit is less than 50 per cent and can be expressed as a simple fraction, then the mark-up can also be expressed as a simple fraction. The mark-up fraction has a denominator which is one whole number lower than the denominator of the gross profit fraction. This is less complicated than it sounds, as will be seen from the following examples:

Examples

	£
Turnover	100
Cost of sales	67
Gross profit	33

Gross profit fraction	⅓	(33 divided by 100)
Mark-up	½	(33 divided by 67)
Turnover	100	
Cost of sales	75	
Gross profit	25	
Gross profit fraction	¼	(25 divided by 100)
Mark-up	⅓	(25 divided by 75)

And so on.

When you are looking at management accounts, bear in mind that the accuracy of the stock figure will have a significant bearing on the accuracy of the gross profit percentage. If stock records are unreliable, if stock has not been properly counted or if the valuation basis is incorrect or slapdash, the reported gross profit and hence the profit percentage will be distorted. Stock is discussed in Chapter 6.

Operating Expenses

The Infallible group has used this heading as a summary for the required analysis. This detail is shown in Table 3.3 below.

Table 3.3

Operating Expenses	*1987*	*1986*
	£	£
Distribution costs	800,000	740,000
Administrative expenses	1,010,000	925,700
	1,810,000	1,665,700

Distribution costs

Distribution costs are the expenses incurred in distributing a company's goods to its customers. Such costs will almost certainly include transport costs of carriage outwards, part of which consists of the wages and salaries of staff working in the distribution department. Selling costs such as the costs of running sales outlets, advertising, wages and salaries of staff working in the marketing and sales departments, and agents commissions will also often be included.

Many privately-owned companies seem to have taken the view that distribution costs only comprise direct transport costs of carriage outwards. In their eyes, all expenses which do not fall under this category, or the category of cost of sales, fall to be classed under the next category of administrative expenses. Once again, it pays to be wary when comparing published accounts of different companies.

However, you have a right to expect the same company to be consistent over a period of time in its treatment of different categories of expense so you can look at trends in distribution costs in the same way that you look at trends in turnover. Look also at distribution costs expressed as a percentage of turnover and compare the changes over a period of time. This is much more informative than looking at distribution costs as absolute figures in isolation. After all, distribution costs ought to be pretty closely linked to turnover.

Example

In the Infallible group's case distribution costs are £800,000 and represent 24 per cent of turnover, calculated as follows:

$$\frac{800{,}000}{3{,}400{,}000} \times 100 = 24\%$$

The comparable figure for the previous year was 25 per cent, which would show that the group has improved its efficiency in this area.

When looking at management accounts, look at each individual item contained within distribution costs in turn. Look at the largest item first. We all know managers who spend 20 minutes discussing fluctuations in the smallest item in the accounts in painstaking detail, and then only have 20 seconds left to skim over the largest or most significant areas of the accounts.

Compare each item of distribution costs with its budget, with the previous period, with trends over the last few periods and with turnover. Try to relate it to other information which you hold. If you know that the company recently switched its business from a cheap carrier to a more reliable but more expensive carrier, do not be surprised if carriage costs increase significantly.

Administrative expenses

In published accounts administrative expenses will often be the dustbin for whatever expenses are left after other costs have been allocated to other categories. Large public companies will try to keep them low by allocating as many costs as possible elsewhere. The directors will not want the shareholders to get the idea that they are spending a great deal of money purely in administration. Spending money on distribution sounds much more productive. Smaller private companies are usually less concerned and are often quite happy for this category of expenses to grow to gigantic proportions.

The Infallible group's administrative expenses have increased from £925,000 in 1986 to £1,010,000 in 1987, an increase of 9 per cent.

When looking at management accounts, follow the same procedure for each item contained within administrative expenses as you do for distribution costs, though bear in mind that many administrative expenses will not vary in line with turnover.

Of course, management accounts may not have a separate section headed: administrative expenses. The costs are more likely to be broken down over more detailed headings or spread over different cost centres. The same principles apply, though.

Expenses

The following are examples of points which may be relevant when looking at individual expenses which do not necessarily vary in line with the current year's turnover:

- Advertising and exhibition expenses – have any campaigns been mounted to increase the next period's turnover? (When looking at this period's turnover, consider what campaigns were mounted in the previous period!)
- Consultancy/sub-contractors – what new consultants have been taken on and what rates are they paid? This figure should also be looked at in conjunction with payroll costs as individuals are sometimes switched from one basis to another.
- Insurance – has the cover been increased? Is the cover adequate?
- Motor expenses – consider changes in the size of the car fleet.
- Rent – does the profit and loss account charge reconcile to the levels of rent set out in the leases?
- Payroll expenses – consider the numbers of joiners and leavers, the last general pay rises and the average amount paid to each employee multiplied by the number of employees.

For all such expenses, of course, the general level of inflation over the period is always useful as a yardstick.

You should also consider whether any items are non-recurring because they arise from special circumstances in the current period. Looked at from another point of view, what special circumstances have there been which *ought* to have given rise to higher or lower expense levels? Have those expected expense levels been reflected in the profit and loss account?

Other Income

Miscellaneous income not derived from turnover is shown

under this heading. In published accounts it is split between up to five categories (see below). The Infallible group's other income is set out in Notes 4 and 4(a) which are reproduced in Table 3.4 below:

Table 3.4

Note 4 Other Income

	1987	*1986*
	£	£
Other operating income	700	–
Income from other investments (Note 4(a))	4,900	5,700
Other interest receivable and similar income	800	–
	6,400	5,700

Note 4(a) Income From Other Investments

Dividends from listed investments	270	260
Rent receivable	4,630	5,440
	4,900	5,700

The five categories are:

Other interest receivable and similar income

This means what it says and will usually consist of interest receivable on bank deposits. You can compare the interest receivable with the average sum on deposit to see if the interest rate makes sense.

Income from other fixed asset investments

If a company owns a small number of shares in another company but the shareholding is not sufficient to make it a group company or a related company (see below), then any income derived from those shares, such as dividends received and any associated tax credit, will be included here.

Income from shares in related companies

We have discussed related and associated companies in Chapter 1. This line will generally only be used in consolidated profit and loss accounts and will show the group's share of the related company's pre-tax profits. If the group owns 25 per cent of the related company then it will bring 25 per cent of that company's pre-tax profits into the group accounts.

Income from shares in group companies

Group companies have also been discussed in Chapter 1. Dividends received from shares in group companies are included in this line of the profit and loss account for the accounts of individual companies. If the accounts are consolidated accounts then this line is redundant because receipts and payments of dividends cancel each other out. In consolidated accounts, the combined turnover, expenses and profits for the group as a whole are shown.

Other operating income

This is a dumping ground for any income that is associated with a company's ordinary activities, but which does not fall under the definition of turnover and does not come within one of the other categories of income. In management accounts you would be provided with full details of any other operating income.

Amounts Written Off Investments

If a business held investments which it had written down from cost or valuation because they had permanently diminished in value, then the amount by which they had been written down in the current period will be shown under the above heading. This does not apply to the Infallible group.

Interest Payable and Similar Charges

This comprises interest paid to banks, hire-purchase companies and so on. Interest payable should be compared to the average borrowings, market rates of interest and the interest rates which have been specified in the borrowing agreements.

The Infallible group's interest payable is analysed in Note 5 to its accounts, which is reproduced in Table 3.5 below.

Table 3.5

Interest Payable and Similar Charges

	1987	*1986*
	£	£
Bank overdrafts	23,000	10,700
Loans repayable within 5 years	400	300
	23,400	11,000

Interest cover

It is impossible to calculate the interest cover for a company. This will show the number of times that interest payable is covered by profits before tax and interest payable. Profits before tax and interest payable are often known as *earnings before interest and tax* or *EBIT*. Interest cover is calculated as follows:

$$\frac{\text{EBIT}}{\text{Interest payable}}$$

Example

The Infallible group makes pre-tax profits of £373,000 after interest payable of £23,400. Its interest cover is very high at 17, calculated as follows:

$$\frac{400{,}000 + 23{,}400}{23{,}400} = 17$$

The comparable figure for the previous year was also 17. This means that interest payable is covered 17 times by EBIT. If EBIT was only £150,000 and interest payable was £100,000, interest cover would be only 1.5, a rather different story!

$$\frac{150{,}000}{100{,}000} = 1.5$$

In such a case a small fall in EBIT of £50,000 would mean no earnings left for shareholders.

Profit on Ordinary Activities Before Taxation

These words are not a legal requirement, but almost every company will draw a sub-total at this point and describe the resulting figure as profit on its ordinary activities before taxation.

At this point, a number of calculations can be carried out on trading profit. We are taking trading profit, for these purposes, to be profit on ordinary activities before taxation and before deducting any interest charges or taking any investment income into account. Any share of the profits of associated companies is also excluded. In other words, to the profit on ordinary activities before taxation is added any interest payable (and similar charges) and any amounts written off investments. Any interest receivable or other investment income is deducted. In certain cases it may be more appropriate to use a different definition of trading profit. The important point is to remember to be consistent when comparing calculations.

Profit margin on sales

Trading profit can be expressed simply as a percentage of turnover, as below:

$$\frac{\text{Trading profit}}{\text{Turnover}} \times 100$$

Example

The Infallible group makes a trading profit of £373,000 on turnover of £3.4 million. Its trading profit is 11 per cent as shown below:

$$\frac{373,000}{3,400,000} \times 100 = 11\%$$

The comparable figure for the previous year was only 6 per cent.

Different industries will make different profit margins on sales, so the precise margin made is mostly of significance for comparative purposes.

Trading profit and employee costs

Where the figure for employee costs is known then trading profit can be expressed as a percentage of employee costs, as follows:

$$\frac{\text{Trading profit}}{\text{Employee costs}} \times 100$$

This will show the sensitivity of trading profit to pay rises and will be particularly significant in companies which provide services.

Example

A company's trading profit happens to be equivalent to its payroll. A 10 per cent increase in its payroll bill will lead to a 10 per cent decrease in trading profit, other things being equal. If its trading profit is only 50 per cent of its total payroll bill then a 10 per cent increase will only lead to a 5 per cent decrease in trading profit.

Trading profit per employee

The accounts will show the number of persons employed by a

company and so it is therefore possible to calculate a figure for trading profit per employee by dividing trading profit by the number of employees. The Infallible group has trading profits of £373,000 and employs 48 people; its trading profit per employee is £7,771. Differences between competitors can be illuminating, although care should be taken in making direct comparisons. One company might, for example, contract out such work as cleaning while another uses its own staff. The trading profit per employee could be lower for the second company even if its cleaning costs were less.

Return on capital employed

Return on capital employed measures trading profit against capital employed, and is calculated as follows:

$$\frac{\text{Trading profit}}{\text{Capital employed}} \times 100$$

Capital employed is normally defined as share capital and reserves (see Chapter 8) together with all borrowings including bank overdrafts. Where there are significant minority interests and deferred liabilities these should be included. From these are deducted, where significant, intangible fixed assets and investments, (including investments in associated companies). This gives the capital employed in trading, that is the capital employed which is relevant to our definition of trading profit. These terms are explained more fully in subsequent chapters.

If capital employed has varied greatly between the start of the year and the end of the year, it would be sensible to take an average figure when making the calculation.

Example

The Infallible group's trading profit is £373,000 and its capital employed is £805,165, made up as follows:

	£
Share capital	10,000
Share premium account	4,000
Profit and loss account	648,000
	662,000
Borrowings	143,165
	805,165

Its return on capital employed is 46 per cent calculated as follows:

$$\frac{373{,}000}{805{,}165} \times 100 = 46\%$$

Based on the average capital employed over the year the return on capital employed was 49 per cent.

If the return on capital employed, however defined, is less than the average interest rate paid on borrowings, something is seriously wrong. The capital employed might be better left in a bank on deposit! The Infallible group does not have this problem.

4

Profit and Loss Accounts – Post-Tax Profits

Chapter 3 took us as far as pre-tax profits on ordinary activities. The next item in format 1 profit and loss accounts is the line which shows the tax charged on that profit.

Tax on Profit on Ordinary Activities

The figure here will represent the total amount of tax which the business will have to pay on the profit it has made on its ordinary activities for the period. The figure is analysed, usually in a note to the accounts, between:

- UK Corporation Tax.
- Deferred taxation.
- UK Income Tax.
- Overseas taxation.
- Irrecoverable Advanced Corporation Tax.

If you are looking at a consolidated profit and loss account which includes the appropriate share of the results of an associated company, the equivalent share of the tax charge for that company will be separately identified.

United Kingdom Corporation Tax

United Kingdom Corporation Tax is the tax which companies have to pay to the UK Inland Revenue on their profits. The current rate is 35 per cent for profits over £500,000; a lower rate of 27 per cent is paid if profits are less than £100,000. There is a sliding scale between. There are additional rules under which companies which are members of groups or are under common control may start paying the full rate of tax at lower levels of profits.

The profit which a company shows in its accounts will only rarely be exactly the profit on which Corporation Tax is charged. This is because various adjustments in accordance with the tax legislation are made for tax calculation purposes to the profits shown in the accounts. These adjustments are not shown anywhere in the accounts so you cannot check the tax charge yourself.

Certain expenses, such as those incurred in entertaining UK customers, are not allowed as deductions for tax purposes. These have to be added back to the profit shown by the accounts before calculating the tax liability. Other adjustments are also made, some of them temporary, some of them permanent. On account of this the charge for UK Corporation Tax on profits of £1 million will rarely equal £350,000.

Deferred taxation

Temporary differences can arise when items of expenditure are allowed for tax purposes in a different year to the year in which they are charged in the accounts. When allowances are given for tax purposes earlier than expenditure is charged in the accounts taxation liabilities can be deferred. This is known as *deferred taxation.* It has mainly arisen in the past as a result of what became known as *accelerated capital allowances.*

The depreciation of fixed assets charged in the accounts is not allowed as an expense for tax purposes; capital allowances are, however, given in lieu. Capital expenditure is charged to profit and loss account under the description of depreciation over periods of between 3 and 10 years in most accounts. In the past, capital allowances (depreciation for tax purposes) had been given on some items at rates as high as 100 per cent. This meant that for tax purposes the cost of the expenditure was all charged in one year.

While such high tax allowances were available in a year when it incurred heavy capital expenditure on plant and machinery, a company paid Corporation Tax on a profit which was much lower when adjusted for tax purposes than the profit shown by its published accounts.

In the next year the company would continue to charge depreciation in its accounts, but it would have no further capital allowances because it would have used them all up. Its tax bill would rise and its tax charge would increase as a percentage of its published profits. Its tax allowances would have been given early – accelerated – instead of being spread over the useful lives of the assets concerned.

The idea of showing an amount for deferred taxation in such instances is to even out the fluctuations in the tax charge caused by differences between the timing of tax allowances, compared with depreciation charged in the accounts. This is done by making provision in the current year for amounts of tax which it is known have only been temporarily deferred and will eventually become payable.

Timing differences between depreciation charged in the accounts and capital allowances given for tax purposes have been used as our example to illustrate why provision is sometimes made in the profit and loss account for deferred taxation. The same principle applies to all other differences of timing between the dates income and expenses are recorded in the accounts and the dates when they are bought into account for tax purposes.

Until the system of giving capital allowances changed on 13 March 1984, accelerated capital allowances was the most striking example of temporary timing differences. The change brought an end to high initial tax allowances on capital expenditure and was phased in over a couple of years. From 1 April 1986 all that companies get in the year when they incur capital expenditure is a tax allowance of 25 per cent of that expenditure. A further 25 per cent on the balance of the expenditure is given in the second year and so on. The tax allowances given may still not be identical to the depreciation charged as an expense in the accounts but the difference is now much less fundamental. The amount of deferred taxation which is charged now in most profit and loss accounts is much less than in earlier years. The amount of Corporation Tax payable on current profits has correspondingly increased.

If you add the charges for UK Corporation Tax and for deferred taxation they will usually be much nearer the expected tax rate than just the charge for UK Corporation Tax. Temporary timing differences will, effectively, have been eliminated and only permanent differences caused by the tax rules will remain.

United Kingdom Income Tax

In addition to Corporation Tax, a company will suffer UK *Income Tax* at the basic rate, currently 27 per cent, on any franked investment income which it receives. Franked investment income consists of dividends from UK companies. Associated with the receipt of a dividend is a tax credit which covers the Income Tax due.

Irrecoverable ACT

ACT stands for Advance Corporation Tax. This is the tax which companies have to pay to the Inland Revenue when they pay dividends to shareholders. It is currently calculated as 27/73 of dividends paid. Companies can, in most cases, set this off against their liability on the company's profits for the year, known as mainstream Corporation Tax. Sometimes though, the ACT will be greater than the tax rules allow to be offset. If there is no immediate prospects of its recovery it will be written off to profit and loss account and disclosed.

Special tax circumstances

A company is also required to disclose any special circumstances affecting its tax liability for the financial year in question or succeeding financial years.

Profit on Ordinary Activities After Taxation

This is what is left of the profit after all tax payable on it has been provided for. It is sometimes known as *earnings* and is the figure which is used, after adjusting for minority interests, when calculating *earnings per share* and, for quoted companies, *the price earnings ratio.* Earnings per share is sometimes known as *EPS* and the price earnings ratio as the *PE ratio.*

Profit Attributable to Minority Interests

This represents that part of the profit of non wholly-owned subsidiary companies which are 'owned' by outside shareholders and not by the parent company. In the case of the Infallible group, the group only owns 75 per cent of the subsidiary company Dellboy Limited. The remaining 25 per cent is owned by outside shareholders. We can assume therefore that the profit of £1,000 attributable to minority shareholders represents 25 per cent of the post-tax profits made by Dellboy Limited.

Earnings Per Share

Assuming that there are no preference shareholders, earnings per share is calculated as follows:

$$\frac{\text{Profit on ordinary activities after tax}}{\text{Number of ordinary shares in issue}}$$

Quoted companies are required to disclose earnings per share on the face of the profit and loss account, so the calculation will be done for you.

You may sometimes see reference made in quoted companies' accounts to earnings per share calculated on a *net basis* and on a *nil distribution basis.* The net basis is the normal basis and takes account of all taxation charges.

The nil distribution basis excludes from the tax charge any irrecoverable ACT or overseas tax suffered because of dividend payments or proposed dividends. The nil distribution basis is thought by some to make earnings per share slightly more comparable as between different companies since EPS on this basis is not affected by differences in their dividend policies. Where EPS calculated on a nil basis is significantly different from EPS calculated on the normal basis, both figures are disclosed. This happens most commonly when companies have large overseas tax charges, such as oil companies.

You may also see reference made to fully diluted earnings. This is relevant where, for one reason or another, additional shares are likely to rank for dividend in the future and will therefore dilute earnings per share at that point. Where such circumstances apply the figure for what earnings per share would have been if such shares ranked for dividend today is also given. It is known as fully diluted earnings per share.

Earnings per share are based on the post-tax profits on ordinary activities and as such do not take into account any extraordinary losses or profits (see below).

It is important to compare earnings per share over a period of time. Is the figure going up or going down? If it is going down, is it because the business is becoming less profitable or is it because more shares have been issued and this has diluted the average earnings per share?

For the Infallible group, earnings per share are £24.20 calculated as follows:

$$\frac{243{,}000 - 1{,}000}{10{,}000} = £24.20$$

The comparable figure for the previous year was £11.20.

Price earnings ratio

For quoted companies, the price earnings ratio is one of the most commonly used yardsticks for judging share prices and values. It shows how many years' earnings per share the share price represents, and is calculated as follows:

$$\frac{\text{Share price}}{\text{Earnings per share}}$$

The price earnings ratio will show how highly the company is rated by the stock market. If one company's shares are priced at 20 times its earnings and another company's only priced at 10, then this is likely to mean that the market rates the former company rather higher than the latter company, but it might mean that the former company had just suffered a bad year and the market expects it to recover.

Extraordinary Items

Extraordinary items are items which derive from events or transactions that fall outside the ordinary activities of the business and which are not expected to recur frequently or regularly. Extraordinary profits, extraordinary losses and any tax attributable should each be shown separately. The tax is not included in the main tax charge on the company's ordinary activities.

Accountants distinguish between extraordinary and exceptional items. An exceptional item is an item which is exceptional by reason of its size, and therefore needs to be disclosed separately in published accounts, but which arises from the company's ordinary activities. Exceptional items are taken into account when arriving at profit on ordinary activities (earnings).

For quoted companies, the whole point of the distinction between exceptional and extraordinary items is that exceptional items affect earnings per share and the price earnings ratio. Extraordinary items do not. To treat something as an extraordinary item is to take it *below the line.* The line is drawn after profit on ordinary activities after taxation, or earnings.

Surprisingly enough, the distinction does have consequences in the real world. The *Financial Times* reported on 26 June 1987 that analysts blamed a fall in the share price of the Argyll Group on its announcement that it was to treat reorganisation costs of some £90 million as an exceptional, rather than an extraordinary item. The share price fell 45 pence in a single day, a fall of 9 per cent from 484 pence to 439 pence! (Actually, Argyll had no alternative if it was to comply with a newly revised accounting standard.)

If part of a business was closed down – one separate division, perhaps – and costs were incurred in closing it down, then these would be regarded as extraordinary. Redundancy costs relating to a continuing division would be regarded as exceptional. The border line between what is normal (although it may be exceptional) and what is extraordinary is often quite difficult to draw. A cynical rule of thumb used by many accountants in such situations – or, more probably, by their or their clients' managing directors – would be that if the item results in a loss it is extraordinary; if it results in a profit then it is normal. This rule of thumb may be cynical, but you will find that in practice it is often quite a good guide. You should look very carefully at any losses which are described as extraordinary. Are they *really* outside the company's normal activities? Do they *really* not recur frequently or regularly? If the answer to either of these questions is 'no', make a mental adjustment to the figure shown for the company's earnings.

Profit for the Financial Year

This is what is left of the profit after all costs have been charged and all taxes have been provided for. (But we will modify this statement when we come to talk about reserve accounting through the balance sheet in Chapter 8.)

Dividends and Retained Profits

A business can either pay dividends to shareholders or it can retain its profit in the business. The next line of the profit and loss account will show any interim dividends which have been paid together with any dividends that the directors propose to pay, and which will have to be approved at the shareholders' meeting which considers the accounts. When a dividend is declared and paid, what the shareholder receives is a net dividend. The company pays the ACT to the taxman and also gives a voucher to the shareholder which shows a tax credit. UK shareholders can treat the tax credit as if it was tax they had already paid. The tax credit is equal to the ACT.

If the directors wish to retain some or all of the year's profits in the business, they will describe that part of the year's profit which is not to be paid out as dividends as retained profit. This will be added to the profits which have been retained from previous years' activities. There is usually no reason why such accumulated retained profits should not be paid out as dividends in the future. If there are any legal restrictions on paying it out then a note will be made as to how much is *non-distributable* (this means that it may not be legally distributed to shareholders in the form of dividends).

Sometimes some of the profit retained in the business for the year will be transferred to a separate reserve for a particular purpose, which will be described (an example might be a 'rebuilding reserve').

Dividend yield

Anyone who owns shares in a company and pays importance to the amount of income received from those shares will be interested in the dividend yield of the shares, and of other available shares. Dividend yield is the gross dividend per share expressed as a percentage of the current share price. It is based on gross dividend because this forms the basis of the taxable income of the recipient. The gross dividend is the net dividend actually paid, plus the associated tax credit. If the figure for gross dividend is not readily available from the accounts it can be calculated easily.

Example

The associated tax credit is currently 27/73 of the net dividend. Net dividend is 11p per share. Associated tax credit is 4.07p, calculated as follows:

$$11\text{p} \times \frac{27}{73} = 4.07\text{p}$$

Gross dividend is 15.07p (= 11p + 4.07p).
Gross dividend yield is then calculated as follows:

$$\frac{\text{Gross dividend in pence}}{\text{Share price in pence}} \times 100$$

Example

Assuming the same figures as before, and a share price of 251p, gross dividend yield is 6 per cent, calculated as follows:

$$\frac{15.07}{251} \times 100 = 6\%$$

Dividend yield can only be calculated when the current share price is known and it is therefore mainly of significance for quoted companies. And when it is significant to them it will also be significant to their managers. It can also be of importance for shareholders of unquoted companies if the value of those companies has to be negotiated with the Inland Revenue.

Dividend cover

Dividend cover is the number of times the dividend per share is covered by the earnings per share and is usually calculated, based on the net dividend, as follows:

$$\frac{\text{Earnings per share}}{\text{Net dividend per share}}$$

Example

Earnings per share are 32p. Net dividend per share is 11p. Dividend cost is 2.9.

$$\frac{32}{11} = 2.9$$

You should be aware that dividend cover becomes more complicated when a company has overseas earnings and suffers foreign tax. Since the foreign tax cannot be set off against UK Corporation Tax, this complicates the amount of dividend which a company could pay out of its profits. The amount becomes restricted. In such cases, dividend cover is calculated on what is known as a *full distribution basis,* as follows:

$$\frac{\text{Full distribution EPS}}{\text{Actual gross dividend}}$$

The full distribution EPS is the maximum gross dividends the company could distribute without eating into its retained profits from earlier years. (How this figure is arrived at is beyond the scope of this book.)

Prior Year Adjustments

There is one final adjustment which a business may make to its retained profits. This is known as a prior year adjustment, which is one which the business makes retrospectively to its retained earnings at the start of the year. It may arise for one of two reasons.

The first is that last year's figures may have been fundamentally wrong. This would be the case if they contained an error of such significance as to destroy the true and fair view shown by the accounts. The normal comparatively minor errors and adjustments which arise in the preparation of accounts do not fall into this category.

If there was a fundamental error it will be corrected, not by adjusting the current year's profits, but by adjusting the comparative figures shown for the previous year and adjusting the sum shown for retained profits at the start of the current year. Full details of the error will be spelt out in the notes.

The second is that a business may have changed an accounting policy. The change may have a significant impact in the level of reported profits.

If there is a change in an accounting policy, last year's figures are similarly restated to show what they would have been if this year's policy had been used. The cumulative effect up to the end of the previous year is shown as a prior year adjustment. The current year's figures are also calculated on the basis of the new policy.

Format 2

The alternative form of presentation for published profit and loss accounts is known as format 2. If the Infallible group had presented its profit and loss account under format 2, the figures for the current year ended 30 September 1987 would look like Table 4.1 below:

Table 4.1

	£	£
Turnover		3,400,000
Changes of stocks of finished goods and in work in progress		15,000
Other operating income		700
		3,415,700

Raw materials and consumables	1,035,000	
Other external charges	50,000	
Staff costs:		
Wages and salaries	427,165	
Social security costs	39,603	
Other pension costs	27,416	
Depreciation and other amounts written off, tangible and intangible fixed assets	21,205	
Other operating charges	1,424,611	
		3,025,000
		390,700
Income from other fixed asset investments	4,900	
Other interest receivable and similar income	800	
		5,700
		396,400
Interest payable and similar charges		23,400
Profit on ordinary activities before taxation		373,000

The presentation of the remaining part of the profit and loss account would have been the same as for format 1.

Format 2 breaks down expenditure by its type, whereas format 1 broke down expenditure by its function. To the extent that format 2 is used, it is used mainly by manufacturing companies although even manufacturing companies divide fairly evenly between those who use format 1 and those who use format 2. Almost all other companies use format 1.

Many of the lines used in the two formats are similar, although they may occur in different places in the profit and loss account, and so we will consider here only those which are unique to format 2.

Changes of stocks of finished goods and in work in progress

This shows the movement between the current year's stock of finished goods and level of work in progress and the corresponding figures for the previous year. If this year's figure is higher than last year's figure, as is the case with the Infallible group, then the difference will increase profits; if the reverse is true it will reduce profits. This item could therefore either be added to turnover or subtracted from it.

Raw materials and consumables

This is the cost of raw materials and consumables after excluding the amount of stock still held at the end of the period.

Other external charges

This is a catch-all which includes items which do not fall under any of the other headings. It will probably include items directly linked to production costs. Payments to subcontractors would usually be included here.

Staff costs

The first line shows gross wages and salaries, the second line shows the employer's social security costs (that is, the employer's national insurance contributions) and the third shows the employer's contribution to any pension scheme which it runs for its staff. Where format 1 profit and loss accounts are prepared, this information has to be given as a note to the accounts. The Infallible group shows this information in Note 21 to its accounts.

Depreciation and other amounts written off tangible and intangible fixed assets

All that is included here for the Infallible group is depreciation which is dealt with in Chapter 5. If long-term investments are written down, then this will also be included here.

Other operating charges

This, again, like other external charges, is a catch-all category. It would include items which were not direct costs of production, were not staff costs and were not depreciation. Most expenses which would be described as administrative expenses or distribution costs in format 1 profit and loss accounts would be included under this heading in format 2.

Other headings

There are also certain other headings in format 2 which do not apply to the Infallible group. These are:

- Own work capitalised.
- Exceptional amounts written off current assets.
- Income from shares in group companies.
- Income from shares in related companies.
- Amounts written off investments.

The last three items also appear in format 1 and do not require any further comment here. The others are discussed below.

Own work capitalised

This item will represent any costs which the company has incurred in manufacturing its own plant and machinery or constructing its own buildings or otherwise building its own fixed assets. The costs incurred would have been charged under one or more of the expense headings below and so the item on this line will represent an addition to turnover. This will have the effect of increasing the company's profits.

Exceptional amounts written off current assets

Current assets comprise stock, work in progress, debtors, short-term investments and bank balances. It would be very unusual for any amount to be written off a bank balance and fairly unusual for exceptional amounts to be written off debtors unless perhaps from third world countries who have stopped payments. More likely than not, any amount included here will be an amount written off stock and work in progress; occasionally, short-term investments will be written down.

Other Formats

In addition to formats 1 and 2, there are two other formats which are also available for published accounts, called formats 3 and 4. However, these are merely horizontal versions of formats 1 and 2. In the old days, both profit and loss accounts and balance sheets were laid out on a horizontal basis. In the case of the profit and loss account, the expenses were shown on the left hand side of the page and the income was shown on the right hand side. (The authors have not seen a published horizontal profit and loss account in the UK for 15 years, and have never prepared one themselves.)

As can be seen from some of our general comments above, whether or not items should be included in specific lines of published profit and loss accounts is sometimes a matter of judgement. Too much should not therefore be read into differences between different companies.

Other Items to be Disclosed in Published Accounts

In addition to the information required to be disclosed in the standard formats, additional information also has to be given in published accounts. Such information is normally given in notes to the accounts. Such items include:

- Rent receivable.
- Income from listed investments.
- Audit fees.
- Cost of hiring plant and machinery.
- Cost of leasing other assets.
- Depreciation charge.
- Net gains or losses in foreign currency borrowings, and whether charged to the profit and loss account or direct to reserves.
- Average number of employees, analysed over appropriate categories.
- Directors' remuneration.
- Remuneration of higher paid executives.

These last two items are usually of interest to most readers of the accounts.

Directors' remuneration

The total figure will be shown, split between fees and emoluments, pensions, and compensation paid to past directors for loss of office. (This last requirement is why golden handshakes have to be disclosed.)

In addition, if total emoluments exceed £60,000, or if the company is a member of a group, there also has to be shown:

- Chairman's emoluments.
- Emoluments of highest paid director, if higher than the chairman.
- The number of directors whose emoluments fall into each £5,000 bracket, but for this purpose pension costs are ignored.
- If any directors waived emoluments, the number who waived them and the total waived (quoted companies also give details of waivers of future emoluments).

The Infallible group disclose directors' remuneration in Note 20 to its accounts.

The total remuneration figure disclosed must include pension costs as well as the estimated money value of benefits in kind. Any sums paid indirectly to a director, such as sums paid to a company controlled by him for the provision of his services, also have to be included. Disclosed total directors' remuneration is therefore usually higher than the total directors' salaries.

In addition to showing directors' remuneration, the accounts will also show details of any loans made to directors. Details will also be given of any other transactions or arrangements involving the company in which a director had, directly or indirectly, a material interest. Group accounts will show such details in respect of directors of the parent company only. No such transactions occurred during the year with directors of Infallible Limited.

Remuneration of higher paid executives

The number of employees, apart from directors, whose emoluments exceed £30,000 has to be shown in bands of £5,000.

Number of employees

A note in published accounts will also give the average number of persons employed during the year analysed over appropriate categories.

By looking at the information given for wages and salaries costs, it is therefore possible to calculate the costs attributable to each employee. Differences between companies in the same industry can be illuminating.

Management Accounts

We will conclude our consideration of profit and loss accounts by illustrating one possible format for management accounts, in summary form.

The table below shows the management accounts for a particular month's trading.

Table 4.2

	Month actual		*Budgeted*		*Variance*	*Same month last year*	
	£	%	£	%	£	£	%
Sales	281,163	100	275,000	100	6,163	252,173	100
Cost of sales	102,463	36	102,000	37	463	95,760	38
Gross profit	178,700	64	173,000	63	5,700	156,413	62
Other variable costs	67,612	24	69,000	25	(1,388)	63,446	25
Contribution	111,088	40	104,000	38	7,088	92,967	37
Fixed costs	83,170	30	80,000	29	(3,170)	75,020	30
Trading profit before interest costs	27,918	10	24,000	9	3,918	17,947	7
Interest costs	2,000	1	2,000	1	–	1,000	–
Net profit before tax	25,918	9	22,000	8	3,918	16,947	7

Management would, in this case, see the current month's actual figures and budgeted figures with the same figures expressed as percentage of sales. They would also see the variances between actual and budgeted figures, both in real terms and percentage terms. Finally, the figures for the same month last year would be shown as an additional comparative.

These summarised figures would be supported by detailed schedules with similar headings showing the break-down of each line in detail. Key ratios would also be included. Very often the manager in charge would append a short narrative offering explanations for variances and stating what corrective action had been taken in respect of adverse variances, when appropriate.

Similar figures would be prepared on a cumulative basis for the year to date (often abbreviated to YTD).

However, there is an infinite variety of ways in which profit and loss accounts could be presented for management accounts purposes, and the particular format used should be one which suits the needs of the company's management.

5

Balance Sheets – Fixed Assets

A balance sheet is a statement of the net assets of a business at a given point in time – a snapshot of the position at the close of business on the last day of the financial year. Assets are the resources which a business owns and which have a monetary cost. Net assets are those resources less sums owed to third parties.

Published balance sheets have to be set out in a standard layout, or format, as it is called. There are two standard formats, format 1 and format 2, but format 2 is merely a horizontal version of format 1 and is rarely used.

Going Concern

As a foreword, it should be emphasised that all balance sheets – and indeed all accounts – are prepared in accordance with an underlying principle called the *going concern concept.* This means that it is assumed that the business will continue in operation for the foreseeable future. It is assumed that it will not have to close down or significantly curtail the scale of its operation. Consider what would happen if the business was forced to close down or sell its assets.

On a forced sale, not all the assets would necessarily realise their balance sheet values. If a business was closed, additional liabilities not recorded in the balance sheet, such as redundancy costs, would almost certainly be incurred.

Under the historic cost convention the value at which assets are recorded in the balance sheet is based on what they originally cost, not their current replacement cost or selling price. The balance sheet values simply represent costs which have not yet been matched against income. Some assets, as we shall see, are recorded in the balance sheet at a valuation, but this is the exception that shows the rule. A balance sheet does not therefore represent the break-up value of a business.

Most businesses of any size will be organised as a group of companies, and the parent company, the company which owns or controls all of the others, will publish two balance sheets. The first will deal purely with its own financial position and will simply be headed, for example *Balance Sheet at 30 September 1987*, or whatever is its year end date. The second will show the total assets and liabilities of the group of companies as a whole, so far as they are owned either directly or indirectly by the parent company, and will be headed *Consolidated Balance Sheet at 30 September 1987*.

The Infallible group's consolidated balance sheet is set out in Table 5.1 below.

Table 5.1

Infallible Limited
Consolidated Balance Sheet
as at 30 September 1987

		1987		*1986*	
	Note	£	£	£	£
Fixed assets					
Intangible assets	9	7,850		2,700	
Tangible assets	10	166,815		154,020	
			174,665		156,720
Current assets					
Stocks	12	500,000		500,000	
Debtors	13	662,000		485,000	
Investments	14	4,550		4,000	
Cash at bank and in hand		450		5,500	
		1,167,000		994,500	
Creditors – amounts falling due within one year	15	656,106		674,180	

Net current assets			510,894		320,320
Total assets less current liabilities			685,559		477,040
Creditors – amounts falling due after more than one year	16	10,559		6,040	
Provisions for liabilities and charges	17	8,000		7,000	
			18,559		13,040
			667,000		464,000
Financed by:					
Capital and reserves					
Called up share capital	18		10,000		10,000
Share premium account			4,000		4,000
Profit and loss account			648,000		446,000
			662,000		460,000
Minority interests			5,000		4,000
			667,000		464,000

A T Green }
P L Stevens } Directors

Approved by the board on
31 October 1987

The top section of the balance sheet is a statement of the net assets owned by the group, and will end with a total which will represent net assets after deducting all liabilities owed to third parties. The second section of the balance sheet, which sometimes starts with the phrase *financed by*, shows the means by which the net assets have been funded.

Balance Sheet Notes

Most published balance sheets will show just the bare bones of a group's financial position. However, a great deal more detail will be shown in the notes to the accounts. Each line of the balance sheet will be cross referenced to its appropriate note. The balance sheet will be contained on a single page; the notes will extend to many pages. Sometimes, many of the most important points are hidden away in the notes.

When reading a balance sheet, the user should look first at the overall picture. This will give the reader a general impression of the company's financial position. Each line of the balance sheet should be looked at in turn compared with the figure for the previous year and reference made to the note to see what additional detail is given.

Certain items of additional detail are required by law in published accounts. Comparative figures for the previous year are given in all published balance sheets and comparative figures are also given for all the detailed figures in the notes. Internal management accounts will often give comparative figures showing both the previous year and the original budget.

Assets are classified as either *fixed assets* or *current assets.* This chapter will deal with fixed assets, the next three with current assets, liabilities, and capital and reserves. We will look first at fixed assets as they are laid out in a published balance sheet. Balance sheets of internal accounts can be produced in any format. They can vary greatly from company to company, although in practice their layout will often follow that of published balance sheets much more closely than is the case with profit and loss accounts.

Fixed Assets

Fixed assets are intended for use in a company's business continuously over a number of years. Such assets are held for the purpose of generating revenue and not for resale. They may be classified as either intangible or tangible fixed assets.

Intangible assets

These are assets which do not have a physical existence. Concessions, patents, licences, trade marks, goodwill and development costs are all examples of intangible assets. Often the most valuable assets a group owns are intangible but are not shown in the accounts. Brand names are good examples. Coca Cola is valued in the accounts of its American owners at US $1!

Intangible assets are required by law to be classified in published balance sheets between:

- Development costs.
- Concessions, licences, patents, trade marks and similar rights and assets.
- Goodwill.
- Payments on account.

Most of these headings are self explanatory, but the headings: development costs and goodwill, require more explanation.

Development costs

Accounting standards require research and development costs to be charged to the profit and loss account in the year in which the costs are incurred. All pure research costs and most applied research and development costs fall into this category. There is an exception for development costs which meet all three of the following criteria:

- They have been specifically incurred on clearly defined projects.
- The commercial success of those projects is reasonably assured.
- The eventual recovery of the expenditure can be regarded as reasonably certain.

Such expenditure may be capitalised and will then slot into the heading, development costs, in the balance sheet. As with other fixed assets, this expenditure is required to be depreciated.

In the case of published accounts, the accounting policy which has been adopted if a business has incurred any development costs will be set out in the list of accounting policies. The notes to the accounts will show the reasons for capitalising the expenditure and the period over which it is to be written off.

In the case of internal accounts further details of the figures, including all expenses charged to development costs, the basis on which they have been charged and how much was charged in the latest month should be available. Details as to when and how the costs are to be recovered should also be available.

Goodwill

When a company buys another profitable company it will almost always pay more for it than the value at which the individual net assets are recorded in that company's balance sheet – their book value. Part of the reason may be that land and buildings are recorded in the balance sheet at figures which are less than their current market values. However, a premium may still be paid over and above that. Such a premium, which represents the difference between the price paid for the company and the value of the total individual net assets acquired, is called *goodwill* by accountants.

The term can be misleading to the non-accountant who may think that it means more than it actually does. *All* it represents is the premium over asset value which has been paid in the past. It certainly does not mean that someone else would pay the same today, or that the figure shown is what the goodwill of the business is worth today.

Goodwill arises in nearly all cases when one company buys another, and it generally appears only in consolidated balance sheets. It will not stay there for ever. An accounting standard dictates that it should either be charged to profit and loss account straight away or should be charged to profits systematically over its economic life – ie depreciated. When premiums over asset value are paid for businesses it is likely to be because those companies are generating more profits than could reasonably be expected from their asset value. Such a situation is unlikely to last indefinitely.

The policy which a group adopts with regard to depreciating goodwill will have a significant effect on its profits for the year. If it writes off goodwill straight away its profits for the year will *not* be affected. This is because the write off will be made against accumulated profits to date, not against the profits for that particular year. If it writes it off gradually over a period of years the charge will be treated as a normal charge against profits. This year's profit and profits for succeeding years will therefore be reduced.

Correspondingly, accumulated profits to date will be greatly reduced if goodwill is written off straight away, but will be shown to be higher if this is not the case.

Due to all these points, the accounts of groups which write off goodwill straight away are really not comparable with those that write it off over a period of time. Extreme caution should be applied if comparisons between companies adopting different policies are attempted. The accounting policy adopted by any group will be set out in its list of accounting policies.

It may be best to view any figure shown for goodwill in a group's balance sheet with some suspicion. Is it justified by profitability? It may be that the subsidiary where the goodwill premium arose is very profitable even though the group's overall profitability is mediocre because other parts of it are loss making. Even so, if the group's overall profitability is only moderate, then what price goodwill?

Remember that goodwill is simply the premium above asset value which the group's management paid in the past for a certain subsidiary or subsidiaries. They may have made a poor decision, or decisions, and have paid well over the odds. So is it still valid to show that premium in the balance sheet today?

One other point on goodwill: a company is not allowed to create its own figure for goodwill assuming it wishes to do so. It can only record in the balance sheet premiums which it has actually paid to a third party in the past. A company may be making profits which are so good that anyone who acquired it would be happy to pay a substantial premium over its asset value; but that is for the potential acquirer to decide, based on the accounts as they stand.

Intangible assets in the Infallible group's consolidated balance sheet are analysed in Note 9 to its accounts and include goodwill, which is being charged to the profit and loss account over a period of five years.

Acquisition accounting and merger accounting

What has so far been written is based on the assumption that when one company buys another, it accounts for it by a method of accounting which accountants call *acquisition accounting.* There is an alternative method which can be used in certain circumstances which is called *merger accounting.*

The differences between acquisition and merger accounting are complex and the mechanics are highly technical. All we can do here is to describe briefly the two main differences in the end results and indicate the circumstances under which merger accounting can be used.

Under acquisition accounting a figure for goodwill will be thrown up in the acquiring company's consolidated balance sheet if it pays more for another company than the fair value of that company's assets. The profit of the acquired company will only be included in the group profit and loss account for the period *after* the date of acquisition.

Under merger accounting no figure for goodwill will arise in the group balance sheet. A premium may still have been paid but it will not show up because it will have been paid in the form of shares. Since an accounting standard requires goodwill to be charged to the profit and loss account (either straight away or over a period of years) the absence of a goodwill figure will mean that this reduction of profits is avoided.

Also, under merger accounting, all of the profits of the acquired company will be included in the group profit and loss account, both for the period *after* and *before* the date of acquisition. Not only is the group avoiding a reduction to its profits by not recording any goodwill to charge against them, it also gets increased profits relating to the pre-merger period into the bargain!

This sounds like a much more satisfactory outcome for the acquiring company! Profits reported under merger accounting are simply not comparable to profits reported under acquisition accounting which themselves are not comparable between groups which adopt different policies towards goodwill. It is a sorry state of affairs.

The basic rules under which merger accounting can be used, can be summarised as follows:

- The acquiring company has to acquire at least 90 per cent of the shares of the acquired company, and at least 90 per cent of the votes.
- The acquiring company must not have held more than 20 per cent of the shares or votes of the acquired company immediately before the offer.
- At least 90 per cent of the total consideration has to be in the form of shares.

Tangible assets

Tangible assets are physical entities such as land and buildings, plant and machinery, office equipment, computers, fixtures and fittings, and motor vehicles. They have to be classified in published accounts under headings which are appropriate to the business.

The following categories are set out in the Companies Act:

- Land and buildings.
- Plant and machinery.
- Fixtures, fittings, tools and equipment.
- Payments on account and assets in course of construction.

These categories are fairly self explanatory. The figures for land and buildings, which are always shown separately from other fixed assets, are split between properties which are freehold, long leasehold (leases with more than 50 years unexpired) and short leasehold.

The Infallible group's tangible fixed assets are set out in Note 10 to its accounts, which is reproduced in Table 5.2 below.

Table 5.2.

Tangible fixed assets

Group and company	*Freehold land and buildings*	*Plant and machinery*	*Fixtures and equipment*	*Motor vehicles*	*Total*
Cost	£	£	£	£	£
At 1 October 1986	128,000	37,000	9,000	6,000	180,000
Additions	–	20,000	4,000	15,000	39,000
Disposals	–	5,000	–	6,000	11,000
At 30 September 1987	128,000	52,000	13,000	15,000	208,000
Depreciation					
At 1 October 1986	*9,920*	*11,320*	*3,240*	*1,500*	*25,980*
Charge for the year	*2,480*	*10,736*	*1,614*	*4,875*	*19,705*
Disposals	–	*3,000*	–	*1,500*	*4,500*
At 30 September 1987	*12,400*	*19,056*	*4,854*	*4,875*	*41,185*
Net book value					
At 30 September 1987	115,600	32,944	8,146	10,125	166,815
At 30 September 1986	118,080	25,680	5,760	4,500	154,020

It is possible to see the amount spent on additions to plant and machinery, and so on, during the year. It is also possible to see the original cost of items scrapped or sold during the year and, from the statement of source and application of funds, the total proceeds received by the business for those items.

If the Infallible group held any assets under hire-purchase contracts (which, strictly speaking, do not belong to the business) these would also be included under tangible fixed assets. The same would apply to assets held under finance leases which are discussed in Chapter 10. The total of these two items would be identified separately in the accounts.

Fixed asset depreciation

Nothing lasts for ever and fixed assets are no exception. They are first recorded in the books of account at cost. The cost is then charged systematically as an expense to the profit and loss account over their useful lives. The estimated useful lives will vary according to the type of asset concerned. The expense concerned is called *depreciation*. Depreciation represents that part of original cost which has been used up in earning revenue. If fixed assets are recorded in the books at a valuation then the valuation is systematically depreciated in a similar way except, as seen below, in the case of investment properties.

Plant and machinery might last 3, 5, 10 years or even longer. The business will estimate how long each class of plant and machinery will last and what it will be worth when its useful life is over. It will charge depreciation in the accounts accordingly.

The original estimate of a machine's useful life can always be changed in the light of changed circumstances or if the original estimate turns out to be incorrect. Newspaper printing presses used to cost a small fortune but with proper maintenance, lasted for a very long time. They might be depreciated over 20 years or more, but then along came the new technology. Overnight, the position changed. The old machinery still worked as well as ever, but was now more of a millstone than an asset.

The calculation of depreciation can often be guesswork. Some of this guesswork has to be disclosed in the accounts. The accounts must show the amount of depreciation charged to the profit and loss account and the basis on which it has been calculated. Some companies show the depreciation rates used and some show the estimated useful lives. It comes to the same thing, provided that the depreciation rate used is applied on a straight line basis. The *straight line basis* simply means that the depreciation rate is applied to the original cost (or valuation) of the asset each year, as in all the examples used in this book.

An alternative method is called the *reducing balance basis*. Under this method the depreciation rate is applied to what is left of the cost (or valuation) after all depreciation charged in previous years has been deducted.

The Infallible group uses the straight line basis and discloses the rates used in Note 1(d) to its accounts.

It is worth looking closely at asset lives disclosed in the accounts to see whether they make sense. If they have been underestimated, depreciation charged to the profit and loss account will be higher than it should be and reported profits will be lower. Correspondingly, the book value of assets in the balance sheet will be on the low side. If fixed assets have been revalued upwards then depreciation based on that valuation charged to the profit and loss account will be higher than it would be if it had been based on original cost; the reported profit will be correspondingly lower.

For internal decision-making purposes, it may be the case that the user is more interested in finding out what it would cost to replace assets when their useful lives are over, than the amount of depreciation charged on a cost incurred some time ago. If the assets are included at replacement cost in management accounts, depreciation charged would also be based on replacement cost. The purpose of the depreciation charge would be not so much to find out how much of the original cost had been used up, as to find out how much is needed to be set aside to replace the asset when it eventually wore out.

Fixed asset valuation

Fixed assets can be included in the balance sheet either at cost or at valuation. Most fixed assets are recorded at cost. The exception is land and buildings, which is quite often shown at a valuation. Where it is shown at a valuation then the corresponding cost will also be shown together with the year in which the valuation was carried out. The accounts will also show the amount that accumulated depreciation would have been if it had been based on original cost. If the valuation was carried out during the current accounting period then the basis on which it was made and the names of the valuers must also be shown.

Most valuations are carried out on an *open market existing use* basis. This means the value which it is thought that someone who did not fundamentally intend to change the use to which the property was put would pay for it.

If there is a substantial difference between the market value and book value of land and buildings, then the directors are required to refer to this in the directors' report (see Chapter 11).

Some categories of land and buildings, known as *investment properties*, are required by an accounting standard to be included in the accounts at their open market value and such assets are then not depreciated. An investment property is a property which is held for its investment value and is not used in the business; it is always separately identified.

All other assets must continue to be depreciated even though they may be included at a valuation; in such cases the depreciation is based on the valuation, not the original cost.

Sometimes a business receives government grants against the cost of fixed assets. The amounts of such grants are either deducted from that cost or are gradually credited to profits over the lives of the assets concerned. An accounting policy should say which method is used.

Fixed asset investments

There is a third class of fixed assets rather inelegantly called *fixed asset investments.* These are investments treated by the directors as long-term holdings not for resale.

Fixed asset investments will be classified as investments in subsidiaries, investments in related companies and other investments. Other investments in turn will be split between listed and unlisted investments in a note. Investments in subsidiaries will not appear in group consolidated balance sheets. The parent company balance sheet of Infallible Limited includes its investments in its subsidiaries as part of its fixed assets.

Table 5.3 below sets out an extract from its balance sheet.
Investments will usually be included in the balance sheet at cost, with aggregate market value being shown as a note. They will normally be written down for any permanent drop in value.

Future capital expenditure

Published accounts also have to show any future capital

Table 5.3

	1987	1986
	£	£
Fixed Assets		
Intangible assets	6,650	900
Tangible assets	166,815	154,020
Investments	39,150	39,150
	212,615	194,070

Investments are further analysed in Note 11, set out below.

Table 5.4

	1987	1986
	£	£
Investments		
Shares in group companies – at cost	39,150	39,150

Name of company and country of incorporation	*Description of shares held*	*Proportion held Direct*	*Proportion held indirect*	*Activity*
Bertie Limited (England)	Ordinary shares	100%	–	Manufacture of colour designs
Cecil Limited (Scotland)	Ordinary shares	100%	–	Designers
Dellboy Limited (England)	Ordinary shares	–	75%	Distribution of colour designs

expenditure if the expense has been authorised by the directors or if contracts have been placed but the assets not yet acquired at the balance sheet date. This will at least give some indication of a company's future capital expenditure programme.

6

Balance Sheets – Current Assets

Current assets comprise cash and other assets which are going to be converted into cash and are not going to be held by a business on a permanent basis.

The current assets of the Infallible group are set out in Table 6.1 below.

Table 6.1

Current assets	*1987*	*1986*
	£	£
Stocks	500,000	500,000
Debtors	662,000	485,000
Investments	4,550	4,000
Cash at bank and in hand	450	5,500
	1,167,000	994,500

Stocks

Stocks are classified in published accounts under three headings. The Infallible group's stocks are set out under these three headings in Note 12 to its accounts, an extract from which is reproduced in Table 6.2.

Table 6.2

Stocks	*1987*	*1986*
	£	£
Raw materials and consumables	85,000	100,000
Work in progress	215,000	175,000
Finished goods and goods for resale	200,000	225,000
	500,000	500,000

All stocks will be included, including stocks on consignment to customers.

Any payments on account which have been received against any items are shown separately as a deduction. This is particularly important for contractors, such as builders.

Raw materials and consumables

For manufacturers, raw materials comprise those items which they buy for use in the manufacturing process but on which no manufacturing operation has yet been carried out. Generally, retail and service companies do not buy raw materials and so they are unlikely to hold any such stock.

Consumables comprise items which are used by a business in the course of its operations but which are not sold by it and which do not form part of the product which it sells. Consumables might include items such as stationery or cleaning materials. Since these have nothing to do with the output of a business they are different in kind from other types of stocks. Such items might be held by all types of business, but are usually insignificant in total and are not often counted. Raw materials and consumables are bracketed together for disclosure purposes in published accounts.

Work in progress

For manufacturers, work in progress comprises goods on which the manufacturing process has been started, but not yet completed. The goods could be at any stage of production. Retailers and wholesalers do not have any work in progress since they do not carry out any operation on the goods which they hold. Companies which sell services could have work in progress, which in their case would consist of costs incurred up to the balance sheet date in commencing work on a service which had not yet been completed.

Finished goods and goods for resale

For manufacturers, finished goods and goods for resale are goods which they have manufactured for sale but not yet sold. For retailers or wholesalers, finished goods comprise goods purchased for resale but not yet sold. Service companies have no stock of finished goods, since they do not sell goods.

Stock Valuation

Stocks are included in published accounts at the lower of cost and net realisable value. They are not valued at their selling price. This is a very important valuation principle and something which it is vital to understand fully.

This valuation basis follows on logically from two fundamental accounting principles. The first of these is the matching principle, which we have already encountered. This states that expenditure should always be matched to the revenue which it generates. Stocks of raw materials represent costs which have been incurred but which have not yet generated revenue, because nothing has been done with them so far. Work in progress represents costs incurred which have not generated revenue because the end result is not yet in a fit state to be sold. Stocks of finished goods and goods for resale represent costs incurred on goods which are ready to be sold, but where no sale has been generated. Stocks of consumables represent costs incurred on items which have not been used in the current accounting period.

While the matching principle states that costs and revenues ought to be matched, the prudence principle states that revenue should not be anticipated before it has been earned. Therefore all that can be done is to carry forward unmatched costs to the next accounting period when they can be matched to revenues which, hopefully, they will then generate.

Therefore all that the figure for stocks included in the balance sheet represents is the carrying forward of costs from one accounting period to the next. That is why they should never be valued at anything higher than cost – to do so would be to anticipate a profit which has not yet been earned.

Costs

The costs at which stocks are valued must be the actual costs which have been incurred and should represent the prices actually paid for the items in question, not what it would cost to buy them new at the balance sheet date, which might well be higher.

Example

A business with a financial year end of 31 December buys 200 boxes of raw materials in June at a cost of £100 per box and still holds 50 boxes at 31 December. Their stock value is £5,000 (50 × £100). This is still true even though the suppliers put the price up to £105 per box in September.

The business also buys one hundred further boxes of the same items in October at £105 per box, and still held ten of these boxes at 31 December. These are valued at £1,050 (10 × £105).

The total stock valuation is £6,050. Two acquisitions of exactly the same raw materials are valued at two different prices, because they cost two different prices.

If a business has hundreds of lines of stock each of which goes up in price once, or maybe two or three times, in the year – and the price rises on different lines of stock may occur at different times – it is not difficult to visualise the practical problems in valuing stocks correctly even with perfect stock records. And to make matters worse, stock records are often much less well kept than other accounting records.

Even if price rises can be identified, how can usage be matched to original deliveries if stock records are unreliable? How do we know that, if we have 60 items in stock, they represent 30 June deliveries and 10 October deliveries, and not some other combination? Various conventions are sometimes used. Some of the more common conventions are set out below, together with the effect which they would have on stock valuation in our example.

FIFO

FIFO (first in, first out) values stock on the basis that stock delivered first is used first. On this basis, the 60 boxes of stock in hand at 31 December would all be valued at September prices since it would be assumed that the June deliveries had all been utilised. The result would be a stock valuation of £6,300 (60 × £105), which would be £250 higher than the true valuation of £6,050.

Average price

Average price takes the average price for each line of stock during the stockholding period. The stocks in our example would be valued at an average price of £102.50 (£100 + £105, divided by 2). This gives a stock valuation of £6,150 (60 × £102.50), which is £100 higher than the true valuation of £6,050.

Weighted average price

Weighted average price takes the weighted average price for each line of stock during the stock-holding period.

The stocks would be valued at a weighted average price of £101.67; this is calculated as follows:

			£
200	×	£100	20,000
100	×	£105	10,500
300			30,500

Weighted average £30,500 divided by 300 = £101.67. This figure gives a stock valuation of £6,100 (60 x £101.67), which would be just £50 higher than the true valuation of £6,050.

LIFO

LIFO (last in, first out) is a very conservative method which always values stock on the basis of the earliest line still held. It would value stock at £6,000 (60 x £100). It is unacceptable in the UK for accounts required to show a true and fair view. It is widely used in the USA.

Replacement price

A method sometimes used for management accounting purposes which is also unacceptable for true and fair view accounts is replacement price. This values stock at what it would cost to replace at the relevant date. For decision-making processes based on management accounts, this is often the most useful measure of value. It would value the stock in our example at £6,300 (60 × £105), assuming no further price rises after September. If there had been a further price rise of £2 to £107 in December then it would use this price and value the stock at £6,420 (60 × £107).

Manufacturing companies

There are additional inherent difficulties for manufacturing businesses in valuing work in progress and finished goods. The values must include the cost of production. How should these costs be allocated? Which overheads should be apportioned and what should the basis be? One such method of establishing costs is *standard cost* which takes costs derived from a standard costing system, and is often used. There are similar problems in valuing work in progress for service companies.

All of the difficulties of valuing stock taken together mean that an element of uncertainty always surrounds the final figure. This is so even when everyone starts off with the best of intentions. In those cases where management's intentions are not quite as pure as the driven snow, they have scope, within broad limits, to manipulate the final stock figure. Estimate piles upon estimate, approximation upon approximation, and the final figure wobbles uncertainly upon those often less than solid foundations. Every £1 increase in the value of stock at the end of the year means an extra £1 of reported profit, and vice versa.

Alternative accounting rules

It is worth noting here that the Companies Act actually permits companies to adopt what are termed alternative accounting rules in the valuation of stock. Under these rules, stock may be valued at its current cost, which would be equivalent to replacement price. Accounting standards, however, do not permit normal categories of stock to be valued on this basis and so this relaxation of the rules in company law is mainly of academic significance.

There are some circumstances under which work in progress is required to be valued at a value higher than its cost, though. This is the case with work in progress held under long-term contracts (see below).

Net realisable value

The prudence principle, in addition to saying that revenues and profits should not be anticipated, also states that provision should be made for losses as soon as they can be foreseen. In some instances, lines of stock and work in progress will have a net realisable value which is lower than their cost. The realisable value of stock is the price at which it could be sold at the balance sheet date in the condition in which it existed at that date. The net realisable value is that price, less any costs which would be incurred in selling it.

The net realisable value of stock may be less than its cost because stock has been damaged to such an extent that no-one would buy it, except at a knock down-price. Stock may have been rendered obsolete by changes in demand caused by changes in technology or changes of fashion. The clothing trade is one instance where changes of fashion can rapidly render stock lines obsolete.

On the other hand, stock may be as desirable as ever to potential buyers but the market price may have fallen to below cost, a phenomenon which has recently occurred in the personal computer market.

In all cases where the potential selling price has fallen below cost price, the prudence principle dictates that the loss which will clearly arise when the stock comes to be sold should be anticipated and provided for in the accounts straight away. In such cases, stock should be written down below cost to its net realisable value. Sometimes, businesses will write down stock below its cost price where none of the factors set out above specifically apply, but where the lines of stock in question are very slow moving. A business may feel reasonably confident that stock will eventually be sold, and that it will be sold at a price which is not less than its cost, but if the stock is slow moving it will often be written down to some extent. This may be justified on the grounds that, because the stock is slow moving, an element of uncertainty exists as to its eventual realisation.

It should always be remembered that, under the going concern principle, a business is assumed to be continuing in operation. The concept of net realisable value should be viewed in the context of disposal of stock in the ordinary course of business. It does not mean what could be obtained on a forced sale, which would probably be lower.

The accounting policy adopted by the Infallible group is as follows:

Stocks

Stocks are stated at the lower of cost and net realisable value. Cost includes all direct costs incurred in bringing the stocks to their present location and condition, including an appropriate proportion of manufacturing overheads.

This is a common form of accounting policy.

Long-term work in progress

Long-term work in progress is work in progress incurred on a contract which will extend over a period longer than 12 months. The construction industry is an industry where such contracts abound. If a company worked on a major contract which extended for a period of five years, and if this was the only contract which the company had, then peculiar results would occur if normal stock rules were followed.

Suppose the costs incurred on such a contract amounted to £10 million, spread over five years, and the final profit on the contract was £5 million at the end of the fifth year. In the first four years of the contract the company would not show any profits at all! In the fifth year a profit of £5 million would suddenly appear. But would it all have been earned then, or would some of it be attributable to work done over the previous four years?

Such situations have prompted the accountancy profession to develop an accounting standard which effectively says that the profit which arises at the end of the contract should be anticipated and spread over the entire period of the contract. Companies are naturally required to be conservative in the way they put this into effect. They are also required to make full provision for any foreseeable losses which may occur on such a contract as soon as such a potential eventuality comes to their notice.

The calculation is done on the following basis. If profits can be foreseen at the end of the contract, a proportion of those profits, which is broadly equal to the proportion of the work done to date, is added to the cost of work in progress. The accounting policy would say something to the effect that long-term work in progress was valued at cost, plus attributable profits after taking into account all foreseeable losses.

Stock to turnover ratio

One of the most popular operating ratios is to compare stocks to turnover and then express the result in months. The calculation is as follows:

$$\frac{\text{Stock}}{\text{Turnover}} \times 12$$

Example

The Infallible group's stocks at the year end are £500,000 and turnover is £3,400,000. Stocks represent 1.8 months turnover, calculated thus:

$$\frac{500{,}000}{3{,}400{,}000} \times 12 = 1.8 \text{ months}$$

The comparable figure for 1986 was 2 months, which shows that the group have become more efficient in holding stock.

Of course, this is not exactly comparing like with like since turnover includes a profit element whereas stocks, except in the case of long-term work in progress, do not.

Stockholding period

A better method is to compare stocks to cost of sales, which can be done in those instances where companies publish their accounts under profit and loss account format 1.

Example

The Infallible group's cost of sales is £1,200,000, and the stock holding period is 5 months:

$$\frac{500{,}000}{1{,}200{,}000} \times 12 = 5 \text{ months}$$

which is rather a different story! The comparable figure for 1986 was 5.2 months.

As with most ratios, the answers are of most value for making comparisons with competitors and with previous years. This is not to say that the management of a business should not wonder about the efficiency of its stock-holding period in absolute terms!

Most companies try to keep a balance between holding the minimum amount of stock necessary to run their business, thereby minimising the amount of working capital which they require (with just-in-time stockholding policies becoming increasingly fashionable), and holding enough stock so that unforeseen shortages are not suffered, with corresponding losses of sales. Again, as with all such performance ratios, it is up to the user of the accounts to decide what he thinks is a good and bad answer. There are no absolute rights or wrongs.

Management accounts ought to identify occasions when stock levels of key items are in danger of falling below the minimum level necessary for the business to operate efficiently. If stock is held at more than one location it may be necessary to identify the different locations.

Readers of management accounts should also be clear how reliable are the underlying stock records on which stock figures in internal accounts are based. When stocks are counted and discrepancies are found between quantities counted and the quantities shown on the stock records, managers should make sure that they understand the reasons for the discrepancies.

Debtors

Debtors are sums of money owed to a business. Debtors are sometimes known as monetary assets, which means that they are assets which will be received in money. In a company's published accounts the figure for debtors shown in the balance sheet will be analysed in a note over various headings. First, the analysis will be between amounts falling due within one year of the balance sheet date and amounts falling due after more than one year from the balance sheet date. Both categories will then be sub-analysed.

The Infallible group does not have any debtors falling due after more than one year from the balance sheet date. Its debtors falling due within one year are analysed in Note 13 to the accounts, which is reproduced in Table 6.3 below.

Table 6.3

Debtors – Amounts Falling Due Within One Year

	1987		*1986*	
	Group	*Company*	*Group*	*Company*
	£	£	£	£
Trade debtors	579,000	481,944	420,000	362,250
Amounts owed by subsidiary companies	–	17,000	–	12,500
Other debtors	31,000	31,000	25,000	25,000
Prepayments and accrued income	52,000	49,000	40,000	38,500
	662,000	578,944	485,000	438,250

Trade debtors

The biggest single category of debtors in most sets of accounts, as it is in Infallible, will be trade debtors. Trade debtors are those sums of money owed to a business for goods supplied by it and services rendered by it. In other words, trade debtors are invoiced sales which have not yet been paid by the customer. As such, trade debtors will include the VAT element of any debt.

If the business has made any payments to its suppliers in advance or has overpaid any suppliers, then these amounts are also usually included in trade debtors.

Any provisions which the business has made against bad and doubtful debts will be deducted from trade debtors, and will be separately identifiable in management accounts but not disclosed in published accounts. Any provisions made for the issue of future credit notes against past sales will also be deducted.

Amounts owed by group and related companies

Any amounts owed to the reporting company by group companies will be shown separately, as will any amounts owed by related companies. Amounts owed by group companies will be self-cancelling in consolidated accounts.

Prepayments and accrued income

Prepayments are expenses paid during the current period which relate to a future period. Usually, each will consist of a proportion of an expense. Most prepayments are time-related expenses required to be paid in advance such as rent, rates and insurance.

Example

A company with a year end of 31 December pays a rates bill of £6,000 before 31 December. The bill covers the half-year from 31 October to 31 March. Of the £6,000 only £3,000 relates to the period before 31 December; the remaining £3,000 is a prepaid expense which will be carried forward under the heading of prepayments.

The composition of prepayments should be examined carefully to see that all items do genuinely relate to future periods and not to the current period. It is a well-known practice for managers to try to carry forward expenditure so as to increase their profits for the current year.

Accrued income is any income which has been earned by the company but not yet been invoiced by it. It is comparatively rare.

Prepayments and accrued income may be shown alternatively as a separate line on the published balance sheet between other current assets and creditors, but this treatment is unusual.

Other debtors

Other debtors will include any debtors which do not fit into any of the other categories! Some companies obtain VAT refunds and any such refunds due at the balance sheet date would be included under this category. A few companies make loans to their directors, which is illegal for amounts over £2,500, and such loans are required to be separately disclosed. Very often they are included under the category of other debtors with a supplementary note stating that other debtors include loans to directors and giving the relevant details.

Foreign currency

Any debtors denominated in a foreign currency are usually converted (the technical term is 'translated') into sterling at a rate of exchange ruling at the end of the financial year, unless a special rate has been fixed. Reference should be made to the list of accounting policies to see the basis of translation. The accounting policy of the Infallible group is as follows.

Foreign currency
Assets and liabilities expressed in foreign currency are translated into sterling at rates of exchange ruling at the end of the financial year. All exchange differences are dealt with in the profit and loss account.

It is certainly worth showing debtors designated in foreign currency separately in management accounts as a way of highlighting and monitoring the uncertainties associated with them. The rate of exchange used should also be shown. In addition to the difficulties in actually collecting amounts owed by overseas debtors, movements in currency rates can mean that the sterling equivalent of the amount finally collected is significantly different from the sums originally intended.

Debt-collection period

Trade debtors can be expressed as a percentage of turnover

which, in turn, can be expressed as a debt-collection period in terms of months. The calculation is as follows:

$$\frac{\text{Trade debtors}}{\text{Turnover}} \times 12$$

Example

The Infallible group's turnover is £3,400,000 and its trade debtors at the balance sheet date are £579,000. Its debt-collection period at that date is 2 months, calculated thus:

$$\frac{579{,}000}{3{,}400{,}000} \times 12 = 2 \text{ months}$$

The comparable figure for 1986 was 1.7 months, which shows that the collection of debtors has deteriorated.

The lower the debt-collection period, the better for the company. This is one instance where absolute rules do apply!

Although it is a most useful ratio, it must still be treated with a little caution. The company's business may be seasonal. If it happens to make only 20 per cent of its sales in the last three months of the year then its apparent debt-collection period will be lower than it really is. For management accounting purposes, it is much better to calculate the debt-collection period by considering sales over the period immediately leading up to the balance sheet date. The calculation is illustrated below:

Example

	£
Sales: October – May	2,720,000
June	272,000
July	136,000
August	136,000
September	136,000
	3,400,000

	£	Months
Debtors at 30 September	579,000	
Less: September sales	136,000	1.0
	443,000	
Less: August sales	136,000	1.0
	307,000	
Less: July sales	136,000	1.0
Balance	174,000	
Balance as proportion of June sales	$\frac{174,000}{272,000}$	= 0.6
		3.6

Debtors at 30 September therefore really represented 3.6 months' sales, which is rather worse than 2 months. The same calculation can be done in terms of weeks or days. Even then, it is still only a guide. It might be that trade debtors of £595,000 include some old April debts still outstanding. The figure of 3.6 months is only an average. (The debt collection ratio can be distorted when companies factor their debts – see Chapter 10.)

Turnover in published accounts excludes VAT whereas trade debtors in most cases include VAT. This is the same for all businesses in the UK, and it therefore has no great significance when comparisons of UK companies are made. If turnover, however, includes a significant element of cash sales or exports, this will distort the ratio since only credit sales give rise to trade debtors and no VAT is charged on exports.

A detailed list of debtors will also be available to managers. Debts will be placed in different columns according to their age in order to make it easy to identify those which are overdue. Each column will also be totalled.

Investments

Investments which are not held on a long-term basis, or for use in the business, are included under current assets in the balance sheet. If they are quoted investments their market value will be noted in published accounts in addition to their cost. This is the case with the Infallible group.

Cash at Bank and in Hand

By convention, the balance shown in the accounts will be the balance shown by the company's cashbook, not the balance shown by the bank statement. Banks do not always agree with this presentation, particularly if it results in an unauthorised bank overdraft appearing in the accounts. The two figures will be reconciled by the company accountant by taking into account cheques drawn and entered in the cash book but not yet presented to the bank, and money paid into the bank and entered in the cash book but which has not yet appeared on the bank statement.

As with debtors, any bank balances designated in a foreign currency should be translated into sterling at the rate of exchange ruling at the balance sheet date.

7

Balance Sheets – Liabilities

Creditors: Current Liabilities and Other Liabilities

Creditors are sums of money owed by a business to third parties. In published accounts they have to be shown on two separate lines on the balance sheet as *amounts falling due within one year* and *amounts falling due after more than one year* from the balance sheet date. Amounts falling due within one year are often referred to as current liabilities. Most creditors which arise in the normal course of trade will fall within this category.

The sums included in amounts falling due after more than one year will usually be loans by banks, hire-purchase companies, finance companies and other lenders. The bank lending to be included under this category will consist of fixed-term loans repayable more than one year from the balance sheet date. Loans repayable less than one year from the balance sheet date, and ordinary bank overdrafts, which are theoretically repayable on demand, will always be included under current liabilities. In addition, any element of a longer-term loan which is repayable in the period within 12 months of the balance sheet date will be split out from the main body of the loan and included in current liabilities.

Example

The Infallible group has a loan of £3,500 which is repayable over the next 7 years at £500 per year. Of this loan, £500 is included in amounts falling due within one year and £3,000 is included in amounts falling due after more than one year. The interest which has accrued on the loan but has not been paid at the balance sheet date is included in other creditors falling due within one year.

The same principles apply to any other loan repayable by instalments.

Further details concerning borrowings will be given in a note to the accounts. All borrowings will be analysed between: (a) amounts payable on demand or within one year (which will be included in current liabilities); (b) amounts payable between one and two years from the balance sheet date; (c) amounts payable between two and five years from that date; and (d) amounts payable more than five years from that date.

It is therefore possible to look at a company's borrowing structure and, taking into account also its capital structure, form a view as to its financial stability having regard to its likely needs for additional working capital, its capital expenditure programme and the dates when fixed-term loans have to be repaid.

The notes to the accounts will further analyse creditors, both those falling due within one year and those falling due after more than one year, into various statutory headings.

The Infallible group's creditors falling due within one year are set out in Note 15 which is reproduced in Table 7.1 below.

Table 7.1

Creditors – Amounts Falling Due Within One Year

	1987		*1986*	
	Group	*Company*	*Group*	*Company*
	£	£	£	£
Debenture loans	500	500	500	500
Bank loans and overdrafts	132,106	132,106	260,180	260,180
Trade creditors	347,000	337,224	295,000	290,350
Corporation tax	112,000	112,000	65,000	65,000
Other taxation and social security	33,550	30,500	26,500	24,750
Other creditors	14,450	13,170	12,500	11,500
Accruals and deferred income	16,500	15,000	14,500	12,500
	656,106	640,500	674,180	664,780

The bank loans and overdrafts are secured by a floating charge over the assets of the company.

Debenture loans

Debenture loans are loans made to the company which are secured on its assets by way of a legal charge. Such charges may be either fixed or floating charges. Fixed charges are fixed on specific assets of the company. Floating charges are not fixed on specific assets but float over certain assets which, by their nature, are likely to change or be substituted in the ordinary course of a company's business. These latter assets might include stock or debtors, the individual items which are, by their nature, constantly changing, although the totals may well remain fairly constant.

Bank loans and overdraft

This is a self-explanatory heading. In published accounts positive bank balances have their own separate line on the balance sheet (together with cash in hand) but bank loans and overdrafts are required to be included, together with all other amounts owed by the business, under the heading creditors. Where a company has both a positive bank balance and a bank overdraft and there is a legal right of set-off, as there usually is, then the positive bank balance will be set off against the bank overdraft and only the net figure will be shown in the published balance sheet. This can have a similar effect on balance sheet ratios to that achieved when debts are factored – see the example in Chapter 10.

It is very common for a bank loan or bank overdraft to be secured on a company's assets. In such a case, and for any other item where security has been given, published accounts will indicate the nature of the security given and the aggregate amount of debts so secured.

In internal accounts, bank overdrafts will invariably be shown separately from creditors, and bank loans will be shown separately from bank overdrafts.

Trade creditors

Trade creditors are the amounts owed for goods and services used by a business in the ordinary course of its trade. As such, they include the VAT element of the original invoice. In most companies, the sums included under the heading, trade creditors, will be the creditors shown on the company's creditors ledger.

Credit payment period

Trade creditors may be compared to cost of sales in the profit and loss account. This can be done where a company adopts the format 1 version of the profit and loss account. This makes it possible to calculate the period of credit being taken by the company from its suppliers. Since trade creditors will usually include creditors in respect of overhead expenditure, a certain amount of caution needs to be applied in interpreting the results, but nevertheless the ratio is useful. It also has to be remembered that trade creditors, as with trade debtors, include VAT whereas cost of sales does not, although this is the same for all UK companies. The ratio is calculated as follows:

$$\frac{\text{Trade creditors}}{\text{Cost of sales}} \times 12$$

The result is expressed in terms of months showing the average period of credit taken by the company.

Example

The Infallible group has trade creditors of £347,000. Cost of sales is £1,200,000. The average period of credit taken by the company is 3.5 months as calculated below:

$$\frac{347{,}000}{1{,}200{,}000} \times 12 = 3.5 \text{ months}$$

The comparable figure for the previous year was 3.1 months, which shows that the group is taking longer periods of credit from its suppliers.

For published format 1 profit and loss accounts the same calculation would be done by adding distribution costs and administrative expenses to the cost of sales. However, one problem could be that certain items which are generally included under these expense headings are irrelevant as far as trade creditors are concerned. The most important of these items is wages and salaries. Any unpaid wages and salaries, or unpaid PAYE or national insurance, would not be included under the heading, trade creditors, so like would not be compared with like.

For published profit and loss accounts prepared under format 2, the following items could be added together and compared to trade creditors:

- Change in stocks of finished goods and in work in progress.
- Own work capitalised.
- Raw materials and consumables.
- Other external charges.
- Other operating charges.

None of these items include staff costs since these are included on a separate line of their own.

The difficulties of finding an appropriate measure of costs from format 1 published profit and loss accounts with which to compare trade creditors, mean that some people compare trade creditors to the company's turnover. There is really no particular logic to this but it can give useful comparative results when comparing different years. It can also be useful for comparing different companies in the same industry where those different companies have similar gross and net profits.

Other creditors including taxation and social security

This heading includes VAT, PAYE and social security deductions and contributions not yet paid over to the Inland Revenue.

It also includes excise duty and ACT payable on dividends. The heading could further include current Corporation Tax and dividends, although such items are normally shown on separate lines of their own. Any items that do not seem to fit in anywhere else also find their way to this category. Note particularly that the amount for current Corporation Tax may not be the same as the amount in the profit and loss account. The balance sheet figure might include Corporation Tax liabilities for two years, or it might take account of payments made for ACT.

Accruals and deferred income

Accruals and deferred income, although shown together in accounts for Companies Act purposes, really consist of two quite different items.

Accruals are really only creditors by another name. A creditor is a liability which has been invoiced and is due for payment at the balance sheet date; an accrual is an item which has not been invoiced separately but where it is known that a liability has been incurred. Accruals will thus often be seen as the opposite of prepayments.

Many accruals will be in respect of time-related expenses such as electricity or gas. If such invoices are rendered quarterly in arrears, as they usually are, then it is likely that the last invoice received by a company before its balance sheet date will relate to a period which ended a little while before.

Example

Infallible Limited has a year-end of 30 September. It receives an electricity bill for £6,000 covering the three months to 31 August, estimates the bill for September as being £2,000, and accrues for it in the accounts under the heading of accruals.

The budgeted figure for time-related expenses is normally used in management accounts as a substitute for the actual figure with variances being dealt with only on an occasional basis.

Some companies include invoices received after the year end and not booked in the bought ledger by the year end under the heading accruals. Other companies include such items under the heading, trade creditors, and only describe as accruals items which are not the subject of separate invoices in their own right. This second course is probably the more correct method. Again, this shows that care must be taken when comparing one company with another.

Deferred income is any income received *before* the balance sheet date which relates to a period *after* the balance sheet date. An example would be where a company invoices in advance for a time-related service, such as a maintenance contract or a year's subscription to a club. In management accounts, any deferred income would be highlighted and shown quite separately from creditors and accruals, with appropriate details being given.

In some companies, instead of being included under the relevant category of creditors, accruals and deferred income are shown on a separate line of the balance sheet; this is an alternative presentation permitted by the Companies Act.

Other headings

There are also certain other headings for the analysis of creditors which do not apply to the Infallible group. These are:

- Payments received on account.
- Bills of exchange payable.
- Amounts owed to group companies.
- Amounts owed to related companies.

Payments received on account

Payments received on account usually relate to payments received on account of long-term work in progress and as such are deducted from stocks and work in progress. However, if payments received on account are greater than the amount of gross work in progress then the excess is included in creditors. If a business can obtain payments on account greater than the cost of the work which it has done, after taking into account any profits attributable to long-term work in progress, it is doing rather well. The heading, payments received on account, does not include part payments from trade debtors if the debtor concerned has made a payment on account of his debt rather than paid the full sum. Such payments are deducted from debtors thereby reducing the amount of debtors shown in the balance sheet. They are not shown separately.

Bills of exchange payable

Bills of exchange are shown separately in the analysis of creditors. Bills of exchange are mainly used by companies for financing international trade.

Amounts owed to group and related companies

Any amounts owed to group companies are shown separately. They are split between amounts owed to subsidiaries on the one hand, and amounts owed to the company's holding company and its fellow subsidiaries on the other. In consolidated balance sheets, these sums are self-cancelling and so do not appear. Amounts owed to related companies will also be shown separately.

Net Current Assets

Total creditors falling due within one year are deducted from total current assets (stocks, debtors, short-term investments and cash at bank and in hand) to give a figure for net current assets. At this point a number of interesting calculations can be made to throw light on the financial position of the business.

Current ratio

The current ratio is a measure of liquidity and gives an initial indication of a company's financial situation, at least in the short term. It is calculated as follows:

$$\frac{\text{Current assets}}{\text{Current liabilities}}$$

Example

The Infallible group's net current assets are as follows:

Current assets	£
Stocks	500,000
Debtors	662,000
Investments	4,550
Cash at bank and in hand	450
	1,167,000
Current liabilities	656,106
Net current assets	510,894

Current ratio

$$\frac{1,167,000}{656,106} = 1.8$$

The comparable figure for the previous year was 1.5.

The ratio ought to be substantially over 1.0 for a financially stable company, but the absolute figure is less important than the trend over a number of years. Is the current ratio getting higher or getting lower? And what are the current ratios for the company's competitors?

Quick ratio

The quick ratio narrows down the current ratio and can give a better understanding of a company's financial stability. It is calculated by eliminating stocks from current assets, as follows:

$$\frac{\text{Current assets} - \text{stocks}}{\text{Current liabilities}}$$

It is often called the acid test. The ratio recognises that the period over which stocks will be converted into cash will often be much longer and less certain than the period over which debtors will be converted into cash.

Example

Taking the Infallible group's figures, the quick ratio is 1.0 as calculated below:

$$\frac{1{,}167{,}000 - 500{,}000}{656{,}106} = 1.0$$

The comparable figure for the previous year was 0.7.

Again, the absolute number is less important than trends and comparisons with other companies in the same sector, although most companies would aim for a quick ratio of at least 1.0. However, there may be other factors at work, and if a company has been happily continuing in business for many years with a quick ratio of much less than 1.0 it will probably be able to continue in business for the future. If a company had a quick ratio of 1.2 two years ago, 1.0 last year and 0.8 this year – then watch out for imminent cash flow problems!

Look at a company's current ratio and quick ratio and consider whether its liquidity position appears to be adequate, bearing in mind any existing loans which may be due for repayment in the immediate future, its immediate capital expenditure programme and its possible need for increased working capital if its turnover is growing.

Working capital

Working capital is stocks plus trade debtors less trade creditors. Working capital can be compared to turnover to see how much working capital is needed to support a given level of turnover. The calculation is as follows:

$$\frac{\text{Working capital}}{\text{Turnover}} \times 100$$

The result is then expressed as a percentage.

Example

Taking the Infallible group's figure, working capital represents 22 per cent of the year's turnover, as calculated below:

$$\frac{500{,}000 + 579{,}000 - 347{,}000}{3{,}400{,}000} \times 100 = 22\%$$

The comparable figure for the previous year was 21 per cent. If the company expects to increase its turnover by 40 per cent next year, this would represent an increase of £1,360,000 and would indicate that it will need further working capital of £299,000 (22 per cent of £1,360,000).

Foreign currencies

All borrowings, bank overdrafts and other creditors designated in foreign currency should be carefully monitored. In published accounts, such liabilities are usually translated into sterling at the exchange rate ruling at the balance sheet date.

In management accounts, liabilities in foreign currency should be separately identified with the appropriate exchange rate noted.

Provisions For Liabilities and Charges

A provision is an estimate of any liability or loss which is certain to be incurred, but where an element of doubt exists as to the actual amount of the liability or loss. In such circumstances the best estimate, made on a prudent basis, should be included in the accounts. Provisions also include any amounts set aside for any liability or loss which is likely to arise but which is not absolutely certain.

Provisions for liabilities and charges are analysed under three sub-headings in a note to the published balance sheet. The headings are:

- Pensions and similar obligations.
- Taxation, including deferred taxation.
- Other provisions.

Pensions and similar obligations

Pensions and similar obligations is a heading which is likely to be used by an increasing number of companies in the future, since many companies now enter into defined benefit pension schemes for their staff. Such schemes define the benefits which will eventually be payable to staff; the total contributions necessary from the company to ensure that the pension scheme has enough assets to pay those benefits are always uncertain. This uncertainty will arise as estimates will have to be made both for future salary levels and investment returns.

Taxation, including deferred taxation

The sub category, taxation including deferred taxation, will usually consist entirely of deferred taxation. Deferred taxation has been discussed in Chapter 4 on the profit and loss account, and a further aspect will be dealt with under the heading revaluation reserve in Chapter 8.

Contingent Liabilities

There is a class of potential liabilities which is not included in the balance sheet known as *contingent liabilities*. A contingent liability is one which may or may not arise, depending upon whether a specified event happens. Such items are only taken up in the balance sheet when they crystallise into actual liabilities. If they are significant in size they will be disclosed in a note to the accounts, unless the possibility of any loss arising is very remote.

Contingent liabilities may include guarantees which have

been given which may or may not be called. Such guarantees would result in a loss if they were called.

If a company is involved in litigation, this may also give rise to contingent liabilities. The management will have a difficult job in satisfying the statutory obligation to disclose contingent liabilities without showing the other side in the litigation, their own assessment of the strength of the case.

Contingent liabilities will be disclosed in a separate note which will usually be found towards the end of the accounts. The Infallible group does not disclose any contingent liabilities.

8

Balance Sheets – Capital and Reserves

Capital and reserves comprise the second section of a balance sheet. The total of a company's capital and reserves in the second section of the balance sheet will equal the total of its net assets in the first section.

Capital and reserves show how the net assets have been funded. This will be partly by the original capital introduced by shareholders, and partly by profits and surpluses generated by the business and retained by it. The latter are known as *reserves*.

Consolidated balance sheets may also have been funded partly by *minority interests*. Where a group of companies is not owned 100 per cent by the parent company, the minority interests in the balance sheet are the proportion of the group's net assets at the end of the year owned by outside shareholders.

The capital and reserves of the Infallible group are reproduced in Table 8.1 below.

Table 8.1

	1987 £	*1986* £
Capital and Reserves		
Called up share capital	10,000	10,000
Share premium account	4,000	4,000
Profit and loss account	648,000	446,000
	662,000	460,000
Minority interests	5,000	4,000
	667,000	464,000

Called up Share Capital

Called up share capital will be analysed further in published accounts, usually in a note, as between the different classes of shares in issue. Different classes may have different rights.

The names given to different classes of share capital are *ordinary shares, preferred shares* and *deferred shares*. Each share is allocated a nominal value which may or may not be the price at which it is issued by the company (this is because shares may be issued at a premium). Shares are not usually issued at a discount. Share structures can become very complex and the particular characteristics of any share will be defined by that company's articles of association.

The bulk of most companies' share capital is comprised of *ordinary shares*. Ordinary shares do not carry fixed dividends. Dividends can vary or be nil. On a winding up, ordinary shareholders are, however, entitled to any surplus capital remaining after all debts and obligations to most other classes of shareholders have been discharged. Most companies only have ordinary shares, but the characteristics of the other shares need to be appreciated.

Preference shares carry rights which have precedence over the rights of ordinary shares in respect of dividends or capital or both. Typically, preference shares are entitled to fixed dividends, but no more, and to a first claim on capital in a winding up. Some preference shares may be redeemable, which means that the capital which they represent may be returned to the shareholders. The shares would then be cancelled under specific terms and conditions and on specified dates.

Deferred shares are shares whose rights to dividends or capital or both are deferred to all or most other classes of shares, normally including ordinary shares.

For each class, the number and total nominal value of allotted shares will be given; the authorised share capital will also be noted. The directors of a company are allowed to issue and allot shares only up to its authorised maximum for each class of shares, although the shareholders can increase this maximum by passing an appropriate resolution.

A company must also give details if it has granted any *options* on any of its unissued share capital. It must state the number, description and amount of shares involved, the period during which the option is exercisable and the price to be paid under the option if it is exercised. Many large companies now give share options to their directors and to senior executives, and it is interesting to see the incentives that have been given in this way. It is also worth seeing how far this will dilute existing shareholders' interests, although the quantum of share options is usually a very minor proportion of total shares, rarely exceeding 10 per cent of total issued share capital.

If any *fixed dividends* of a cumulative nature are *in arrears* then this must also be stated in the notes. This is likely to mean that the company has had a history of losses. Since preference dividends take precedence over dividends on ordinary shares, significant arrears could indicate a long wait for any future dividends for ordinary shareholders.

If there are any *redeemable shares* in issue, the accounts have to disclose the earliest and latest dates of redemption, and whether redemption is mandatory or at the company's option or the shareholders' option. They also have to show the premium, if any, which is payable upon redemption. If mandatory redemption at a significant premium is imminent then this could make great financial demands upon a company.

If any shares have been allotted in the year, the details together with the reasons for the issue will be noted in the accounts. This may give an indication of the company's future intentions.

Reserves: Non-Distributable Reserves

Reserves are either distributable or non-distributable. A distributable reserve is a reserve which has been realised and where there is nothing in law to prevent it from being distributed to shareholders as dividends. A non-distributable reserve is a reserve which may not be so distributed.

Share premium account

If shares have been issued for a price which is higher than their nominal value, then the excess of the price they were issued for over their nominal value is included in the balance sheet under the heading: share premium account. Share premium account is non-distributable and is treated for most practical purposes as being identical to share capital.

Revaluation reserve

Land and buildings are sometimes included in the accounts at a valuation higher than their original cost. The recognition of this increase in value is shown as a revaluation reserve. It is not taken to the profit and loss account. It is non-distributable since it has not been realised. There may be tax to pay if such an unrealised reserve is subsequently realised.

The Infallible group owns freehold land and buildings which the directors have stated in their report has a market value of £50,000 more than the value in the accounts, ie a total value of £165,000. This is an increase of £37,600 over cost which would be taxable if the property was sold. If the accounts at 30 September 1987 had shown the property at a valuation of £165,600 a revaluation reserve of £50,000 would have arisen. If the company had foreseen a subsequent sale it would have provided for the potential tax liability by reducing the revaluation reserve by the amount of tax payable. This tax liability would be shown as deferred taxation under the heading of provisions for liabilities and charges.

If the company had no present intention of selling the property then it would make a note of the potential tax liability which would arise if the property were sold. Such a note would normally be placed at the foot of the note to the accounts dealing with the deferred taxation. Sometimes properties can be sold without any tax liabilities arising because of a tax relief called rollover relief; in such cases the fact that no tax liability arises will be stated.

Other reserves

If any of the three following reserves arise then they would be included under the heading of other reserves and details shown in the notes to the accounts:

- Capital redemption reserve.
- Reserve for own shares.
- Reserves provided for by the articles of association.

A *capital redemption reserve* arises where a company has redeemed or bought in part of its own share capital. It is created so that total capital is not thereby diminished. In order to create it, a sum is transferred from profit and loss account. Capital redemption reserve is undistributable and is treated for most purposes as being identical to share capital. When a company buys in part of its own share capital its distributable profits are reduced to the same extent.

Distributable Reserve

Profit and loss account

This will show the accumulated undistributed profits to date after taking into account all taxation liabilities based on those profits. Many companies call this item *revenue reserve*. It will be linked to the retained profit for the year shown at the foot of the profit and loss account in a note to the accounts. Such a note will start with the accumulated profit at the start of the year, will add on the profit for the year and may then make certain adjustments for items which are not charged to the profit and loss account. Such items might include adjustments arising from certain exchange rate conversions and the writing-off of goodwill.

Unless a note to the contrary is given, retained profits at the end of the year are realised profits which the company may distribute as dividends to its shareholders.

Shareholders' Funds

Shareholders' funds comprise capital and reserves. These will normally be called up share capital, share premium account, revaluation reserve and profit and loss account. The total is equivalent to the net assets of the business (apart from any minority interests) and is also known as the net worth of the business.

Minority Interests

The figure for minority interests represents the proportion of the net assets of subsidiaries owned by outside shareholders.

The Infallible group owns only 75 per cent of Dellboy Limited, the remaining 25 per cent of that company being owned by other shareholders. We may infer that minority interests of £5,000 at 30 September 1987 represents 25 per cent of the net assets of Dellboy Limited.

Debt/equity ratio

Having reached the end of the balance sheet, it is now possible to calculate the *debt/equity ratio*. This shows the proportion of funds provided by third parties as compared with ordinary shareholders and minorities. It is usual to deduct any intangible assets from shareholders' funds. It is also usual to take only ordinary shareholders' funds into the calculation. The calculation is as follows:

$$\frac{\text{Preference share capital} + \text{loans} + \text{bank overdraft}}{\text{Shareholders funds} - \text{preference share capital} + \text{minority interest} - \text{intangible assets}}$$

Example

The Infallible group's consolidated balance sheet has shareholders funds of £662,000 comprised of:

	£
Ordinary share capital	10,000
Share premium account	4,000
Profit and loss account	648,000
	662,000

Total borrowings are £143,165.

Its debt/equity ratio is 22 per cent calculated thus:

$$\frac{143{,}165}{662{,}000 + 5{,}000 - 7{,}850} \times 100 = 22\%$$

Some people might express this as a ratio of debt to equity of 1:4.6.

If the proportion of debt to equity is high then the company is said to be *highly geared*. If it is low, as in our example, then the company has *low gearing*.

It is important to note that the definition of this ratio which we have given would not be used by everyone. Some people would take preference share capital as being part of equity. Some people would do that if the preference shares were irredeemable but exclude them if they were redeemable. Some people would exclude minority interests from equity. The exact definition is not that important: it depends on what you want to know. The definition of the debt/equity ratio could be expressed more simply as:

$$\frac{\text{Debt}}{\text{Equity}}$$

and each person can then make his own definition of debt and of equity.

Net asset value

Net asset value is the value of assets attributable to each ordinary share. The assets are taken at their balance sheet value. It is calculated as follows:

$$\frac{\text{Ordinary shareholders' funds}}{\text{Number of ordinary shares issued}}$$

Ordinary shareholders' funds are arrived at by deducting from shareholders' funds classes of share capital other than ordinary share capital. The Infallible group has ordinary shareholders funds of £662,000 and a called up ordinary share capital of £10,000. The net asset value of each share is £66.

9
Funds Flow Statements

Before a new business can start trading, an appropriate level of funds is required. Initial funds will come in the form of business capital provided by the proprietors – share capital in the case of a company, sometimes together with a proprietors' loan. Other people may be pursuaded to make long-term loans to a business to provide further initial funds.

Why is the money needed? Fixed assets and stock need to be purchased. There will be wages and overheads to be paid before the first sale is made. The first few months of trading are unlikely to generate any significant amounts of revenue. There will be a waiting period before cash is received from customers to whom sales have been made on credit terms. The debts owed to the business will have to be funded.

The promoters of a new business should have calculated the need for initial funds on a basis to take all these factors into account and on the assumption of a certain level of activity and turnover. Once a business has reached this level, additional funds will be required if it is to expand. Where will these funds come from?

There are a number of possibilities. Additional funds could be made available from the proprietors; in the case of the company, additional share capital could be issued. New long-term, medium-term or short-term borrowings could be arranged. A business could increase its bank overdraft facility, with the consent of its bankers. Finally, if a business is profitable, it will generate funds of its own in the form of the profits which it makes.

A business which has been in existence for a number of years could also generate funds by selling surplus fixed assets. An established business is also likely to have more scope than a new business for generating funds from its trade creditors by taking longer periods of credit, although there is obviously a limit. An established business which has become slack in collecting amounts due from its debtors can also generate funds by speeding up the process of debt collection.

But where does the money go? It might be used to purchase additional fixed assets or stock or to finance a higher level of debtors. It could pay off some of its short-term, medium-term or long-term liabilities. It could purchase investments. It could pay increased dividends to its shareholders. It could pay off its trade creditors more quickly in the hope of enhancing its reputation with its suppliers, or it could afford to give a longer period of credit to its own customers. It could simply use its funds to build up its own cash mountain.

Not all of these possibilities are necessarily good, but they all exist. It is important to know which of them have been followed. The balance between inflows and outflows is crucial. The information will not be available from the profit and loss account for the period or from the balance sheet at the end of the period.

Far more companies go out of business for want of funds or for misuse of funds than for want of profits. The simplest way to present flows of funds is to summarise cash inflows and cash outflows. This has been done for the Infallible group for the year ended 30 September 1987 in Table 9.1 below.

Such a descriptive statement of inflows and outflows of cash is accurate but limited in the information it gives. It has the disadvantage that not being linked to profits it does not show what funds have been generated from profits. Furthermore, while it shows the total sums received from debtors and paid to creditors it is not possible to tell from it whether the level of debtors is increasing or decreasing, and similarly for creditors.

Table 9.1

	£	£
Inflows		
Receipts from sales		3,691,000
Receipts from borrowings		4,519
Receipts from fixed asset sales		11,000
Receipts from proprietors		–
		3,706,519
Outflows		
Payments for supplies and expenses	3,042,311	
Payments of wages	494,184	
Purchase of fixed assets	47,000	
		3,583,495
Decrease in cash balance	(5,050)	
Decrease in bank overdraft	128,074	123,024

Statement of Source and Application of Funds

In order to overcome these difficulties, accountants have developed a financial statement with the rather unwieldy title of a *statement of source and application of funds*. They have also developed an accounting standard to go with it. All companies with a turnover of more than £25,000 per annum have to include such a statement with their published accounts. The statement has to be audited. The Infallible group's statement of source and application of funds is set out in Table 9.2 below.

We will conclude this chapter by showing how to easily link profit to changes in the cash resources of the business.

Table 9.2

Infallible Limited,
Statement of Source and Application of Funds
for the Year Ended 30 September 1987.

	1987 £	£	*1986* £	£
Source of funds				
Profit before taxation		373,000		179,000
Extraordinary item before tax relief		(57,000)		–
		316,000		179,000
Items not involving the movement of funds:				
Depreciation	21,205		15,200	
Profit on disposal of fixed assets/1986:Loss	(3,150)		2,100	
		18,055		17,300
Funds generated from trading		334,055		196,300
Other sources				
Proceeds from disposal of fixed assets	11,000		10,500	
Proceeds from loans falling due after more than one year	4,519		–	
		15,519		10,500
Total funds generated		349,574		206,800
Application of funds				
Purchase of fixed assets	47,000		24,000	
Tax paid	65,000		103,000	
Dividend paid	–		100,000	
		112,000		227,000

Net inflow of funds				
1986:Outflow		237,574		(20,200)
Increase/(Decrease) in working capital				
Debtors	177,000		120,000	
Investments	550		–	
Creditors	(63,000)		130,000	
		114,550		250,000
Movement in net liquid funds:				
Cash and bank balances	(5,050)		10,020	
Bank overdraft	128,074		260,180	
		123,024		270,200
		237,574		(20,200)

The first part of the statement deals with sources and applications of funds. The second part deals with changes in working capital.

Sources of funds – where did the money come from?

The first section starts with the profit before taxation as shown on the profit and loss account. This figure is then adjusted for any items which obviously do not involve the movement of funds. Depreciation, which is an expense which is not linked to the outlay of money, is always added back. Any loss on the sale of fixed assets is added and any profit on such a sale is subtracted. A sub-total is then drawn which represents funds which the business has generated internally from its operations.

Funds from other sources

Added to the funds which the business has generated from its own trading operations are any further funds which it has obtained. They might come from its proprietors, from long-term loans or from other sources. Other sources might include funds from the disposal of fixed assets, in which case the actual proceeds are shown. A sub-total is then drawn of the total sources of funds during the period.

It is standard practice to exclude from this section items which are not permanent. These are shown in the second part of the funds statement dealing with working capital.

Applications of funds – where did the money go?

The items set out under this section include amounts spent on the purchase of fixed assets, payments of tax, payments of dividends or for the repayment of medium-term or long-term loans. Again, it is standard practice to exclude from this section any items which are not permanent. These are shown in the second part of the funds statement dealing with working capital.

When the total applications of funds are deducted from total sources the resulting figure shows by how much working capital has increased or decreased.

Movement in working capital

This forms the second part of the statement and is split into two sections. The first section shows the changes in stocks, debtors, creditors and any other non-cash current assets. The second section shows the movement in cash and bank balances, known as the movement in net liquid funds.

An increase in working capital is an increase in stock, debtors or cash at bank; a decrease in working capital is an increase in creditors or bank overdraft.

In conclusion, the statement effectively shows what permanent sources of funds the business has had during the period, what permanent uses it has made of them, what other permanent outflows there have been, and how the net inflow or outflow has been reflected in changes in working capital. Working capital is stock, debtors, short-term investments and cash balances less creditors and bank overdrafts – net current assets, in fact!

Using the Funds Statement

The funds statement included in published accounts helps you to see how profit generated by the company has been used, and also where other money which it has managed to obtain has been spent. Has it been used in purchasing fixed assets for the long-term benefit of the business, or perhaps for a future expansion programme? Has the money been used to repay long-term borrowings? How much has gone in paying tax to the government? How much have the proprietors taken as dividends? The money might have been used to fund higher levels of stocks and debtors. Obviously, higher levels of stocks and debtors will need to be funded somehow if a business is to grow.

The relationship between profits and funds generated from other sources can be illuminating, as can the uses to which those funds have been put.

Suppose stock levels have increased significantly. What is the change in the stockholding period ratio? Have stocks increased because the level of business has increased? Is too much stock being held? Perhaps stock levels have deliberately been built up for an anticipated increase in future business, or because key stock items might soon be in short supply, or to ward off the effects of a future price rise. Whatever the reason, you can see it has an effect on liquid funds.

If a company has made a loss and, even after adjusting for depreciation, has lost funds through its trading activities, it is possible to see how the loss of funds has been financed.

10

What Might Not Appear In Accounts

In a court of law, a person under oath is required to tell 'the truth, the whole truth and nothing but the truth'. Users can feel fairly sure than an audited set of accounts will tell the truth and nothing but the truth. But will the accounts tell the whole truth?

Exclusions

The problem is that sometimes some items are excluded from accounts. Such items are not missed out because they have been forgotten; they are excluded because they concern transactions which have been cleverly designed to be allowed by law to be omitted. It may even be unlawful to include them. Many of these transactions concern various methods of what is known as *off balance sheet financing.*

Off balance sheet financing arrangements fall into two broad categories. Under the first, companies obtain the use of assets in return for incurring obligations to make payments for the use of those assets for a period extending far beyond the balance sheet date. The obligations are structured in such a way that the companies do not have to show those obligations (or the assets) in their balance sheets. Under the second category, companies or groups obtain the use of funds in such a way that they are not required to show the source of those funds in their balance sheets.

Companies are not required to show those obligations or sources of funds (let us be bold, and call them both liabilities) because the arrangements are highly complex legal constructions, specifically written with that end in mind. There is a considerable and continuing demand for such schemes. They are highly popular with managers and it is easy to see why. After all, why show liabilities when you can avoid doing so? Such schemes represent brilliant triumphs of legal form over economic substance, and are much liked by lawyers.

Accountants, who generally show less finesse in such matters, feel awkward when they confront such schemes. Their whole training leads them to believe that substance should take precedence over legal form. Being spoilsports, they think that all liabilities ought to be included in the balance sheet.

Some of the forms of off-balance sheet financing arrangements, which have recently been popular are financed through:

- Leasing arrangements.
- Non-consolidated subsidiaries.
- Controlled non-subsidiaries.
- Associated companies.

Changes, however, can be rapid as new schemes are conceived.

Additional forms of off-balance sheet financing which have been undertaken in recent years, though not necessarily solely for the purpose of obtaining off-balance sheet finance, are finance from debt factoring, and finance from discounting bills receivable.

Leasing arrangements

The attraction of leasing arrangements has largely fallen away following developments on two fronts. First, changes in the tax regime have made leasing arrangements less financially attractive to both lessors and lessees. Second, accountants developed an accounting standard which forces lessees to include the liabilities arising under such arrangements in their balance sheets. As most lessors are banks and similar institutions, we will only deal here with the effect on lessees' balance sheets.

Before the development of the accounting standard a company could obtain the use of an asset for its entire useful economic life by leasing it. But because legal title to the asset was never obtained, both the asset and the liability to make the payments that went with it were excluded from the balance sheet. The accounting standard, with which most lawyers disagree, defeats the objective of obtaining off-balance sheet finance, by distinguishing between two types of leasing arrangements. The first type is called a *finance lease*, and the second an *operating lease*.

Under a finance lease the person who leases the asset (the lessee) enjoys more or less all the rewards of ownership and takes more or less all the risks. The lessee will be able to use the asset over substantially all its useful life. The commitments taken on by the lessee are roughly equivalent to what they would be if the lessee had purchased the asset and paid for it steadily throughout its useful life. In such a case, the asset will rarely be leased to any other party once the lease has expired.

An operating lease is any other form of lease. Typically, an operating lease would be a lease over a period of time substantially shorter than the useful economic life of the asset with payments amounting to correspondingly less than the cost of the asset. Often, the responsibility for the maintenance of the asset remains with the lessor. With a finance lease it is usually the responsibility of the lessee.

The accounting standard, which is mandatory for all accounting periods beginning on or after 1 July 1987, states that liabilities under finance leases should be taken up in the balance sheet in the same way as all other liabilities, and that the corresponding assets should be capitalised as fixed assets. Obligations under operating leases are not taken up in the balance sheet. The amounts to be paid under operating leases over the 12 months after the balance sheet date are, however, disclosed, appropriately analysed.

Although finance lease liabilities do not have to be taken up in balance sheets for accounting periods beginning before 1 July 1987, the obligations under those leases have been disclosed in a note to the accounts for all accounting periods which began on or after 1 July 1984. This is another example of notes being of vital importance when looking at published accounts.

Non-consolidation of subsidiaries

Group accounts are usually required to include all companies. In certain circumstances, individual subsidiaries can, however, be omitted from the consolidation. One is where the activities of a subsidiary are so dissimilar to those of other group companies that consolidated accounts would be misleading and the information would be better provided by presenting separate financial statements. All the group has to do is take the subsidiary into the group balance sheet on a one-line basis, as if it were an investment in an associated company.

The published group accounts then have to include the separate accounts of the omitted subsidiary. These have to include details of the parent company's interest, particulars of amounts owed to and by other group companies, the nature of transactions with other group companies and a reconciliation of the separate accounts with the group investment in the omitted subsidiary shown in the consolidated balance sheet. The details given in the separate accounts for the omitted subsidiary are often, in practice, rather less complete and informative than might be desired.

It is therefore open for a group to hive off into a separate subsidiary all the credit facilities which it provides to its customers. Those credit facilities will probably be financed by bank loans and borrowings by the subsidiary. If the subsidiary is omitted from consolidated accounts all those bank loans and borrowings will also be omitted from the consolidated balance sheet. In other words, the group can obtain funds from which to provide its customers with credit facilities but omit the source of those funds from its consolidated balance sheet. But this is not the end of the story.

Contingent liabilities

Using a hived-off subsidiary seems quite a clever idea. But what happens if the hived-off subsidiary makes losses and cannot pay its liabilities? The group as a whole is unlikely to be able to walk away. Almost certainly it will have had to guarantee the repayment of those liabilities to the institutions who provided the funds. If the subsidiary cannot itself pay its liabilities, then the rest of the group may well have to do so in its place.

Guarantees of this sort have to be fully disclosed in the group's accounts under the note which discloses the group's contingent liabilities.

It is important to look very closely at the note which discloses contingent liabilities to pick up items such as this. As a rule of thumb, the longer and more complicated the note, the more you should worry! Your worry quotient should also increase in direct proportion to the size of the figures in the note, even though the note may explain that the contingent liabilities arise in the ordinary course of business.

Controlled non-subsidiary

A company is a subsidiary of an investing company if the investing company holds more than 50 per cent of its voting equity share capital or, even if holding only one share, controls the composition of its board of directors. It is possible to arrange matters so that the investing company holds shares in a company which falls outside the definition but is still effectively controlled by it.

One way to do this is to own 49 per cent of the shares with a further 49 per cent held by a friendly merchant bank. It is arranged that the remaining 2 per cent of shares are held by a non-associated friendly party, possibly a charity or trust. The investing company holds an option to purchase the bank's shares should it so wish; the bank holds an option to *require* the investing company to purchase those shares. If profits are made, the investing company will purchase the shares whenever it suits it. If losses are made, the bank will force the investing company to purchase the shares straight away! Such an arrangement will probably allow the investing company to control the other company effectively without having to consolidate it as a subsidiary. It will take it into the group balance sheet on a one line basis as an associated company.

As with the case of a non-consolidated subsidiary, finance

could be arranged through this non-subsidiary company with the corresponding liabilities being excluded from the group balance sheet. No doubt those liabilities would have to be guaranteed and, once again, reference should be made to the note concerning contingent liabilities.

One common use of a controlled non-subsidiary is for borrowing against properties. A trading company might wish to borrow directly on a property, but if it did so the full liability would be disclosed on its balance sheet with the corresponding effect on its debt/equity ratio.

In order to avoid this, the trading company could arrange a sale of the property and agree to rent it from the purchaser over a period following the sale and thus retain its use. This is known as a sale and leaseback. The disadvantage with this arrangement is that at the end of the rental period the property is no longer available to the trading company.

The sale and leaseback could instead be arranged with a controlled non-subsidiary which would borrow the full amount required from a financial institution. The immediate effect is the same to the trading company – the sale proceeds are received and rent is payable.

At the end of the period the trading company will still have control over the property, which might well have increased in value. The liability to the financial institution may well also remain, but will have remained constant in money terms. The trading company's debt/equity ratio, however, will not at any time have been affected yet the company will not have lost the opportunity to enjoy the growth in the value of the property.

Associated company

It is possible for an associated company to incur liabilities which are excluded from a group's consolidated balance sheet but guaranteed by it. Again, reference should be made to the note on contingent liabilities in the group's accounts.

Factoring of debts

A company can sell the debts its customers owed to it to a

factoring company for immediate cash. This can be either with or without recourse. On a without-recourse basis, when a customer does not pay the factoring company suffers the loss. On a with-recourse basis, when a customer does not pay the factoring company does not suffer the loss. This is because it claims it back from the supplier company which therefore suffers the loss itself.

The usual practice when debts are factored is to deduct cash received from the factoring company from the amount of debtors shown in the balance sheet. If factoring is without recourse, then no further disclosure is required. If it is with recourse, a contingent liability exists in respect of debts from customers where the company has received cash from the factoring company, but where the factoring company is still awaiting payment from the customer. The amount concerned will be indicated in the note on contingent liabilities.

Apart from this note, which could easily be missed, there would be no indication of a company's method of financing its debtors. How different things might appear if a bank overdraft had been used instead!

The way that debtors are financed can have a quite significant effect on ratios, as shown in the following example:

Example

A company has current assets, excluding stocks, of £400,000 and current liabilities (including a bank overdraft of £200,000) of £300,000. Its quick asset ratio would be 1.3 as calculated below:

$$\frac{400{,}000}{300{,}000} = 1.3$$

If it factored debts of £200,000 and paid off its bank overdraft its current assets would be reduced to £200,000 and its current liabilities would be reduced to £100,000 giving a quick asset ratio of 2.0 calculated thus:

$$\frac{200{,}000}{100{,}000} = 2.0$$

By reducing both the top and bottom of the fraction by £200,000, the quick ratio has been increased significantly, and the balance sheet made to look that much stronger.

Discounting of bills receivable

Bills receivable can be discounted for immediate cash in the same way that debts can be factored.

Published accounts

The ways to find out from published accounts about the existence of off-balance sheet financing is to look very closely at the list of accounting policies and at the note on contingent liabilities, guarantees and other commitments.

If you are looking at group accounts, look at the list of accounting policies to discover the basis of consolidation adopted. Be on guard if it says that certain subsidiaries have been omitted. For both groups and individual companies, look at the accounting policy for accounting for leased assets. If it does not say that assets held under finance leases have been capitalised and the appropriate leasing commitments taken up as liabilities there is another reason to be on guard. However, not all companies use leases and so there may not necessarily be anything untoward by no reference to leased assets being made at all in the list of accounting policies.

Look very closely at the contingent liabilities note. Published accounts are required to show all contingent liabilities and all guarantees. They are also required to show details of any security given in respect of them. When assets have been given as security for liabilities of other companies then that will be disclosed. This may well be the only hint you will receive from the accounts of the existence of some methods of off-balance sheet financing and of what liabilities will crystallise if any such fancy schemes go wrong! The longer, more complex and more incomprehensible the note, the more you should be on guard.

Management accounts

The simple message when considering management accounts is this, 'Do not kid yourself'. You can omit liabilities from the balance sheet, but they will not go away. They will still be there. You will probably have to pay them one day. It is the economic substance of the transaction which counts. Legal niceties are not very helpful when you are trying to run a business.

11

Directors' Reports and Chairman's Statements

Companies will publish an annual report of the directors to accompany the audited accounts. Quoted companies will also publish a chairman's statement together with, in many cases, a chief executive's review of operations. Non-quoted companies will rarely produce anything in addition to the directors' report.

The main purpose of these reports and statements is to add to the information given elsewhere in the accounts.

Directors' Report

There are a number of matters which are required by law to be dealt with in the directors' report. Perhaps the most important of these concern the principal activities of the business, its development during the year and its prospects. The directors' report is also the right place to look for details on research and development policies, the market value of land and buildings, and particulars of the directors themselves.

The directors' report of the Infallible group is reproduced in Table 11.1 below.

Table 11.1

Infallible Limited

Report of the Directors

The directors present their report and accounts for the year ended 30 September 1987.

DIRECTORS

The directors who served during the year were:

A T Green
Mrs B White
P L Stevens
W A Brass

W A Brass retires by rotation and, being eligible, offers himself for re-election.

PRINCIPAL ACTIVITY AND REVIEW

The principal activity of the group throughout the year has been the manufacture and distribution of colour designs.

The results for the year and the financial position at the year end were considered satisfactory by the directors who expect continued growth in the foreseeable future.

FIXED ASSETS

Details of changes in the fixed assets are shown in the attached accounts.

In the opinion of the directors the freehold land and buildings has a market value of £50,000 in excess of the amount shown in the accounts.

DIRECTORS' INTERESTS

The directors had the following interests in the shares of the company at the beginning and end of the year:

A T Green	2,000
Mrs B White	2,000
P L Stevens	1,000
W A Brass	500

RESEARCH AND DEVELOPMENT

The group continues its policy of investment in research and development in order to maintain a competitive position in the market.

DONATIONS

The group made charitable contributions during the year amounting to £1,500.

DIVIDENDS

The directors do not recommend the payment of a dividend.

FUTURE DEVELOPMENTS

Approval has been given for the construction of a new factory which is expected to be completed by the summer of 1988; this will increase the group's production capacity by 20%.

AUDITORS

A resolution will be submitted at the annual general meeting proposing that Tried, Tested & Co. be reappointed auditors and that their audit fee for the ensuing year be agreed with the directors.

A T Green
31 October 1987 Chairman

Principal activities

The directors are required to state the principal activities of the company or group during the year, together with any significant changes which have been made to those activities in that period. It may well be interesting to read this information in association with details of turnover and profits for different classes of business given in the notes to the accounts.

Business review

A potentially very important requirement is for the directors to include in their report a fair review of the development of the business during the financial year and of its position at the end of the year. In the case of a group, this review encompasses the businesses carried on through subsidiary companies. The words 'fair review' are both broad and bland. It is open to directors to decide how much detail they wish to include. Many large quoted companies will go into considerable detail. However, since the contents of the fair review section of the directors' report will often overlap considerably with what they would otherwise write in the chairman's statement or chief executive's review of operations, they might merely say in the directors' report that the fair review of the business is included in one of those other documents.

The directors' report, as well as dealing with the development of a business through the year, is also required to give particulars of any important events which have occurred after the balance sheet date. If a company had bought or sold another business after the balance sheet date, this would certainly be an example of an event to be disclosed. Other than that, what is, and is not an important event open to judgement, but at least we are talking about events which have actually occurred.

Future developments

The next requirement is for directors to indicate likely future developments in the business of the company, and, where appropriate, its subsidiaries. Here, we have moved away from the area of what has happened, which at least is factually based, to the area of what will happen, which, in the real world, is probably anyone's guess. All the directors can do is state what they intend to happen, or what they think is likely to happen. Again, firms of accountants have developed stock phrases such as 'the directors expect to see continued growth in the foreseeable future' for use by smaller companies.

Research and development activities

The directors are required to give an indication of the research and development activities of the company and its subsidiaries. The accounts themselves are required to give very few details in this area. Unless development costs are capitalised, the only information which the accounts proper will provide is the disclosure of the accounting policy adopted. Usually, this merely says that research and development costs have been charged to profit and loss account.

The amount spent on research and development does not have to be disclosed anywhere. Most companies spend money on research and development in order to obtain a commercial benefit. It is not an academic exercise. One might well think that the future success of many companies will depend, in the long run, on their success in this particular area.

Fixed assets

Directors are required to note the nature of significant changes in fixed assets during the year. Often, they will simply refer to the note on fixed assets in the main accounts. They are also required to indicate, as precisely as they can, any substantial differences between the market value of interests in land owned by the business and its book value if, in their opinion, the difference is of such significance that it should be drawn to the attention of the shareholders. This information can be extremely useful for anyone trying to establish the real asset value of a business. Land and buildings bought years ago are likely to have increased substantially in value but may not have been revalued in the balance sheet.

Directors

Directors have to give details about themselves. The names of all persons who served as directors during the year have to be shown. For those who were still directors at the end of the year, any interests which they had in the shares of the company, or any group company, at the end of the year and at the beginning of the year (or the date when first appointed a director, if later) have to be disclosed. Details do not have to be given in the accounts of a wholly-owned subsidiary for a person who is a director of both it and its holding company; in such instances details are given in the holding company.

Dividends

Directors must state the amount of the dividend they recommend and of the profit which they intend to transfer to reserves.

Employee information

Additional information has to be given by companies where the average number of UK employees was more than 250 during the year. For such companies, the directors are required to state their policies on the employment of disabled persons. They are also required to state what actions they have taken during the year as regards employee involvement in the affairs of the business.

Political and charitable contributions

If the total exceeds £200, the separate totals of contributions for political and charitable purposes made during the year have to be disclosed. The total of these can be compared to the total profits made by the company. For individual donations of more than £200 made for political purposes, the name of the recipient has to be disclosed. Donations made to persons or parties outside the UK will not be shown. The requirement does not apply to wholly-owned subsidiaries of UK parent companies.

Purchase of own shares

Appropriate details must be given by all companies which have actually acquired their own shares during the period.

Quoted companies

Certain other disclosures have to be made by both listed and unlisted (USM) companies on the securities market:

1. Directors have to state whether, so far as they are aware, the company is a 'close company' for taxation purposes.
2. If any person other than a director has an interest of 5 per cent or more of the nominal value of any class of share capital carrying voting rights, details have to be disclosed. Directors may choose to disclose the position as at any date, not more than one month before the date of the notice of the shareholders' meeting at which the financial statements are to be presented.
3. Details of any contract of significance between a group company and a corporate substantial shareholder have to be disclosed. Details also have to be given of any contract for the provision of services to the company by a corporate substantial shareholder unless the provisions of such services is the

shareholder's principal business and the contract is not one of significance.

4. Particulars of any authority given by the shareholders, enabling the company to purchase its own shares, if the authority is still in effect at the year end, must be disclosed.

5. Any change in directors' interests between the end of the financial year and a date not more than one month before the date of the notice of the general meeting at which the accounts will be presented.

6. For a listed company, but not for a USM company, further details concerning directors will be shown.

Chairman's Report and Chief Executive's Review of Operations

All large quoted companies include a chairman's report, and many include a chief executive's review, or something similar. These will usually be right at the front of the glossy brochure which is produced. They are usually distinguished by a very bright and attractive layout, with many photographs, in comparison with the drab presentation of the main accounts.

The information contained about the business can be extremely useful. The business is likely to be broken down into its constituent divisions with the activities, progress and future plans of each division set out in some detail. In particular, the products or services which lie at the centre of the business are likely to be fully described. For someone who wants to find out what the business actually does, rather than discover its financial results, these are the pages to head for. If you think that the products or services of the business are of a high quality, or are of great potential, or are based in growth areas, then this may be more important in its implications for the future than the results for the past set out in the accounts. Certainly, the key strategies adopted by a business are likely to be explicitly set out in such statements.

However, a note of caution should be sounded. Any figures contained in the statement are not audited and a chairman may well dwell on the more upbeat side of the business and pay less attention to areas of risk.

The name of a business may be unfamiliar to you, but the names of some of its major products may give you more clues as to what the business is all about. Descriptions of its major products will almost certainly be given prominence in these statements. Household name products, however, the names which stick in the mind, may represent only a minor part of the business as a whole, so an element of caution is called for. In any event, the fact that a product is a household name does not mean that the business which sells it is sound.

The names of key executives below director level who are responsible for the management of important divisions may also be given. This can be useful information if you are keeping a watching brief on an industry. You can also look at the remuneration details of anonymous higher paid employers (which are given in notes to the main accounts) in order to get an idea of their salaries.

12
Audit Reports

The annual published accounts which companies in the UK have to send to their shareholders are required by the Companies Act, as we have seen in Chapter 1, to give a true and fair view of the profit for the year and of the state of affairs at the end of the year. They also have to be presented correctly and to disclose certain specific information. The responsibility for ensuring that the accounts do this is laid upon the directors.

However, since the directors will have had complete control over the reporting company's financial management during the year, they can hardly be viewed as being independent. For this reason, the Companies Act requires the accounts to be independently audited. After they have completed their audit, auditors are required to issue a report to shareholders giving their opinion as to whether the accounts show a true and fair view and whether they comply with the Companies Act.

This applies to all companies, limited or unlimited, public or private, quoted or unquoted.

An audit of a company's accounts is an independent examination of those accounts. The audit will cover the company's accounting records and the whole system of financial and other controls established by the directors to safeguard the company's assets. The controls will ensure that the accounting records, from which the accounts are prepared, are accurate and complete. The auditors have a legal right of access to all the company's books and vouchers. They also have the right to require directors and other officers of the company to provide such information and explanations as they require for audit purposes.

Auditors

The key requirement for an auditor is independence. The Companies Act prohibits directors, employees and other officers of a company from being auditors of that company. Persons who are partners of, or in the employment of, such people are also so prohibited. Auditors are not allowed to be companies; that is why all audit reports are signed either by individuals or partnerships. Most auditors work in partnerships which vary in size from 2 partners to 400 or more. They may employ anything from a handful of staff to over 5,000. Over and above these statutory restrictions, auditors should be, and be seen to be completely independent and free of any interest which might detract from their objectivity.

Auditors are also required to be suitably qualified. A person who is not suitably qualified is not allowed to act as a company auditor. Most auditors are either 'Chartered Accountants' or 'Certified Accountants'. Certain individuals who hold foreign qualifications regarded as being of equivalent standard may on individual applications, also be authorised by the Department of Trade to act as auditors. There are, in addition, a number of auditors who were in practice with suitable experience before 1947 who are individually authorised by the Department of Trade.

Auditors are appointed annually by a general meeting of shareholders, although, in practice, the appointment is usually strongly influenced by the directors.

The auditors' report is attached to accounts sent to shareholders and filed on public record. In the case of modified accounts filed by small and medium-sized companies, the audit report on the full non-modified accounts is filed, even though the full accounts themselves are not filed! A report to the directors by the auditors confirming that the company meets the criteria allowing it to file modified accounts also has to be filed.

The fact that directors have prime responsibility for ensuring that accounts give a true and fair view and comply with the Companies Act is often overlooked, because, unlike the auditors, they do not have to confirm this in writing on the face of the accounts. Their confirmation, however, that this is so is implicit in the signatures of the two directors who sign the accounts on behalf of the board of directors.

Unqualified Audit Reports

Auditors have developed a standard form of wording to signify their opinion that accounts on which they are reporting are, indeed, true and fair and comply with the Companies Act. Such a report is called an *unqualified opinion.* This means that the auditors have no reservations about their opinion.

The following is the standard form of wording:

Report of the auditors to the members of Cecil Limited.

We have audited the accounts on pages 3 – 14 in accordance with approved auditing standards.

In our opinion the accounts give a true and fair view of the state of the company's affairs at 30 September 1987 and of its profit and source and application of funds for the year ended on that date and comply with the Companies Act 1985.

Tried, Tested & Co
Chartered Accountants
77 Audit Row
London EC1
31 October 1987

We will look at the form of this report in more detail.

Heading

The heading to the report merely identifies to whom it addressed, the members (shareholders) of Cecil Limited.

Scope

The first paragraph of the audit report, known as the scope paragraph, sets out the scope of the audit. The first part identifies by page numbers the accounts on which the auditors are reporting. This is quite important since, in the case of a large quoted company, audited accounts may account for less than half of the large glossy brochure sent to shareholders. Any information which falls outside the numbered pages referred to in the audit report has *not* been audited.

The directors' report and chairman's report will not have been audited, although auditors are required by law to say if anything in the directors' report is inconsistent with the audited accounts. Other than that, they have no obligations, and no rights to comment on any other material in the brochure in their audit report. Despite this, they do have a right to speak at shareholders' meetings on any business which concerns them as auditors. If they believed that information contained in other parts of the glossy brochure was factually incorrect or misleading they could exercise that right to speak.

Since auditors have this right they are usually able to persuade directors to omit any misleading or incorrect information they might otherwise be tempted to include. It is certainly in the auditors' interest to do so lest their name might be tarnished by association.

The second part of the scope paragraph reveals that the audit has been conducted in accordance with approved auditing standards. This is a reference to a set of auditing standards which have been issued during the 1980s by the leading accountancy bodies which codify, in broad terms, current best audit practice.

Opinion

The second paragraph of the auditors' report is known as the opinion paragraph. It says, without any reservations, that the auditors' opinion is that the accounts are true and fair and comply with the Companies Act.

Termination

The report ends by giving the name and address of the auditors. (Some large firms of auditors consider themselves to be so well known and prestigious that they merely give their address as 'London'.)

The report is also dated, indicating the date when the audit was concluded. This date can be significant since auditors will not have been able to consider any events after that date which might give additional information of relevance to the accounts. Watch out for accounts containing audit reports dated months before you receive them.

Qualified Audit Reports

Any auditors' report which is longer than the two paragraphs of the standard unqualified audit report is likely to be a qualified opinion. This means that auditors do have reservations as to whether the accounts are true and fair, and/or whether they comply with the Companies Act. Qualified audit reports will follow the same general pattern as unqualified reports. They will start with a scope paragraph and finish with an opinion paragraph. However, there will be an additional paragraph (the explanatory paragraph) in the middle to spell out the reasons why the opinion is qualified. Wherever possible, auditors are required to quantify the effect in figures. The final paragraph, the opinion paragraph, will then set out the extent of the qualification.

Different degrees of reservation are possible, and auditors have code words which signify both the type and the degree of their reservations. Reservations fall into two broad categories: disagreement and uncertainty. Both types of reservation can be either fundamental or material (that is, significant and important but not fundamental). These subjective judgements will be based on the auditors' professional experience.

We will explain in the next few paragraphs how to recognise the four main types of qualifications:

1. Fundamental disagreement (adverse opinion).
2. Material but not fundamental disagreement (codeword: except for).

3. Fundamental uncertainty (disclaimer).
4. Material but not fundamental uncertainty (codeword: subject to).

Fundamental disagreement

Where auditors disagree with the view given by the accounts on a matter which is so fundamental as to undermine the view given by the accounts as a whole, they give an adverse opinion. After the scope paragraph, the explanatory paragraph will set out the circumstances of the disagreement. The opinion paragraph will then begin with words similar to 'because of the significance of' the matter referred to in the explanatory paragraph 'in our opinion the accounts do not give a true and fair view' of the company's profit, state of affairs or source and application of funds.

When it is said that accounts do not give a true and fair view, this is the strongest qualification possible. Such qualifications are rare, perhaps because the threat of one leads companies to change accounts so as to avoid it. Any accounts in respect of which such a qualification does appear are more or less worthless.

Nevertheless, such a report may go on to say that 'in other respects (or, 'except for the matter set out above') the accounts in out opinion comply with the Companies Act'. This sentence appears because auditors remain required by law to report on compliance with the Companies Act in other respects even when they do not think that the accounts give a true and fair view.

A material but not fundamental disagreement

Where auditors can isolate the matter on which they disagree to a specific aspect of the accounts which is not so fundamental as to undermine the view given by the accounts as a whole, they will start the opinion paragraph with the phrase 'except for'. They will then refer to the matter set out in the explanatory paragraph. This is auditors' code to indicate disagreement, but also to indicate that the view given by the accounts as a whole is not fundamentally wrong. Where able to do so, auditors will quantify the effect of their disagreement.

A frequent example of an 'except for' opinion occurs where accounts have been prepared on a basis which does not comply with a relevant accounting standard.

Uncertainty

The two previous types of qualifications arose where auditors disagreed with the view given by accounts.

Qualifications arise from uncertainty in cases where auditors, for one reason or another, are unable to form a view, either on the accounts as a whole, or on a particular aspect of them. It is not, or should not be because the auditors have opted out. It will be because there are inherent uncertainties as to the relevant facts or circumstances. There are insufficient facts to enable a considered opinion to be reached.

Fundamental uncertainty

In some instances, auditors may decide that there are so many uncertainties, or that there is an area of such fundamental uncertainty that they are unable to express any opinion at all on the accounts. Such areas of fundamental uncertainty will be set out in the explanatory paragraph of their report.

The opinion paragraph of the audit report will then start by saying 'because of the significance of the matter referred to in the preceding paragraph we are unable to form an opinion as to whether the accounts give a true and fair view. . . .'

Limitations on scope of audit

Fundamental uncertainty sometimes arises where limitations have been placed on the scope of auditors' work. This will mean that they have been unable to obtain all the information and explanations they want. This would be the case if, as happens from time to time, some or all of a company's records have been destroyed.

If limitations of any sort have been placed on auditors' work, the scope paragraph will be expanded so as to qualify the reference to approved auditing standards as follows:

We have audited the accounts on pages 3 – 14. Our audit was conducted in accordance with approved auditing standards except that the scope of our work was limited by the matter referred to below.

The explanatory paragraph will then set out details of the limitation.

If auditors have been unable to form an opinion as to whether proper accounting records have been kept they will say so in the opinion paragraph. They will say this in addition to their disclaimer of opinion as to the view given by the accounts.

Material but not fundamental uncertainty

The code phrase which auditors use to describe such a situation is 'subject to'. This phrase will be used at the start of the opinion paragraph, and will refer to areas of uncertainty set out in the explanatory paragraph. It will say something along the lines of: 'subject to the effect of any adjustment which might have been shown to be necessary'.

Examples of such a qualification often occur where companies are involved in major unresolved litigation.

Management assurances qualifications

Many small businesses receive what are popularly known as management assurances qualifications. These are given where there is a lack of evidence as to the operation by the company of proper controls over some or all transactions. This might mean that transactions could be omitted from the books and therefore from the accounts. In such cases, the explanatory paragraph of the qualified audit report will say something along the lines of:

In common with many businesses of similar size and organisation, the company's system of control is dependant upon the close involvement of the directors, who are the major shareholders. Where independent confirmation of the completeness of the accounting records was therefore not available, we have accepted assurances from the directors that all the company's transactions have been reflected in the records.

The opinion paragraph will then say 'subject to the foregoing, in our opinion the accounts give a true and fair view. . . .'

Many people have come to accept this as something less than a qualified opinion. This is not the case. The opinion is as qualified as any other 'subject to' opinion arising from a material element of uncertainty surrounding the accounts. To put it bluntly, by giving this opinion auditors are expressing uncertainty as to whether all transactions have been reflected in the accounts. This might be because of a significant element of cash sales without corresponding controls over the cash. The auditors would then in effect be saying that they were unsure whether all cash sales had been included in the accounts. Such a qualification is unlikely to cause a great deal of concern to banks or suppliers, provided that amounts owed to them were otherwise regarded as secure; however a shareholder who was not a director might find the qualification worrying.

Multiple qualifications

Sometimes, a qualification will contain elements of both uncertainty and disagreement to a material but not fundamental extent. A 'subject to' opinion may be combined with an 'except for' opinion. It is very difficult for auditors to combine these two elements and still write clear English, and the results are usually obtuse.

CCA accounts

An exception to the rule of thumb, that any audit report longer than two paragraphs is likely to be a qualified report, occurs where quoted companies produce supplementary current cost accounts in addition to historic cost accounts. In these cases, the first two paragraphs will follow the usual format except that the opinion paragraph will identify the historic cost accounts by their page numbers.

There will also be an additional paragraph at the end of the report which will give an opinion as to whether the supplementary current cost accounts (which, again, will be identified by page number) have been properly prepared.

Group Accounts

Audit reports on group accounts will refer to the state of affairs of both the company and the group at the balance sheet date because group accounts contain two balance sheets, one for the parent company and one for the group. However, they will refer only to the profit and source of application of funds of the group, and not of the company, since separate figures for the parent company are not disclosed.

Fraud

One final point needs to be made. Auditors do not consider that it is their responsibility to detect or prevent frauds. Auditors are quite clear that the responsibility for preventing fraud, or for detecting it should it happen, lies with the directors. It is up to the directors to do this by setting up an appropriate system of financial and other controls. Auditors are clear in their own minds that they do not have a duty specifically to search for frauds in the normal course of events. The general public do not always share this view.

However, if a fraud, or other irregularity, was so material as to distort the reported profit for the year or to distort the balance sheet at the end of the year, auditors would expect to find out about it. If they did not, their audit opinion on truth and fairness of the accounts would rest on shaky ground.

Quoted Companies Half-Yearly Figures

Quoted companies are required to issue half-year summary profit and loss accounts to shareholders. These figures will be described as unaudited.

Unaudited Accounts

Accounts either have or have not been audited. There is no

half-way house. If accounts have not been audited then the reader is completely reliant upon the competence and integrity of the accountant who prepared them. Unaudited accounts, when prepared by a suitable person, may well be reliable. Indeed, a qualified accountant who knew his job would not expect significant adjustments to be made to his accounts by auditors. Nevertheless, the comfort of an independent opinion is usually worth having.

When prepared by an incompetent or otherwise unsuitable person, unaudited accounts can be misleading, or wrong, or both.

13

Checklist

During the course of this book, we have explained what particular items in the accounts represent, how they are valued and how they can be used for planning, controlling and decision-making. We have done this for each item as we have come to it in the profit and loss account, balance sheet, funds flows statement, directors' report, chairman's report and chief executive's review of operations. In this final chapter we summarise some of the main themes, and hints, in understanding company accounts.

1. When you first look at a set of accounts, you may be overwhelmed by a mass of figures, so ask yourself a few questions:

- What matters am I going to decide, if any, on the basis of reading these accounts?
- What information do I therefore need, and how precise does it have to be, to assist me in making those decisions?
- What information do I need to enable me to monitor the implementation of those decisions?
- What information do I need to be able to monitor the implementation of decisions taken in the past?

2. When looking at published accounts read and understand the audit report. If it is qualified remember to reread it when dealing with that part of the accounts to which the qualification refers.

3. Look at the totals shown in accounts first. Get your bearings. Next, look at each line in turn. Then look at the more detailed information shown in the note or schedule to which the line is referenced.

4. Get your company accountant to summarise key figures for you on a single page. If this is not possible, do it yourself.
5. Do not forget that some areas of accounts are surrounded by inherent uncertainty. Do not insist on or expect spurious accuracy for such figures.
6. Decide in advance to what extent you are prepared to sacrifice accuracy to timeliness. If the profit shown by your company's audited accounts is significantly different from the profit shown in its management accounts, insist on seeing a reconciliation between the two figures. If it is found that the management accounts contained significant errors review any decisions which have been taken on the basis of that incorrect information.
7. When reading management accounts, if a figure differs from what you think it should be, or does not seem to make sense, then query it. Ask for a breakdown; find out what business transactions the figure is supposed to represent. Errors do occur.
8. Compare the current period's figure to the figure for the previous period and consider what the trends have been over the last five years. Look at these trends in terms of percentages, although there is no need to bother with decimal points, at least in the first instance. Especially examine the profit trend.
9. If you are looking at management accounts, pinpoint fairly precisely where variances have arisen. Who is responsible? Why has it happened? Are the variances due to internal or external factors?
10. When you see losses shown as extraordinary items in a company's profit and loss account look carefully at the description of those items. Are they really outside the company's normal activities? Do they really not recur frequently or regularly? If the answer to either of these questions is 'no', make a mental adjustment to the figure shown for the company's profit on ordinary activities.
11. Look carefully at any intangible assets which are disclosed in a company's balance sheet. Goodwill and development costs are prime examples. Are these items really justified? Do they really have an economic worth?
12. Most consolidated accounts are prepared on the basis of

acquisition accounting. When you see accounts prepared on the basis of merger accounting, remember that profits are likely to be much higher than they would have been on the more usual basis of accounting. Nothing, however, has changed, apart from the accounting convention used.

13. On what basis have land and buildings been included in the balance sheet. Is it cost or valuation? If at a valuation, what was its basis and when was it carried out? How different do you think that the value would be today on the same or a similar basis? If looking at published accounts, see whether the directors have made any comment in the directors' report as to differences between the book value and market value of land and buildings.

14. What asset lives have been used for depreciating fixed assets? Do they make sense?

15. Look at the basis on which stock and work in progress has been valued. Remember that this area of the accounts is always a matter of approximation. Remember also that each additional £1 of stock at the end of the year means an additional £1 profit for the year.

16. Look at the basis at which assets and liabilities designated in foreign currency have been translated into sterling. Consider whether there have been any significant exchange rate movements since the balance sheet date.

17. Look at the repayment schedule for loans. How much is repayable in the next year, in years two to five, or after year five? What funds are or will be available, to make the repayments?

18. Look at provisions for pension scheme obligations and deferred taxation. How much is shown to be payable and how much is likely to be payable? What funds are available?

19. Look at the company's capital structure.

20. Look for clues as to liabilities omitted from the accounts, such as various methods of off-balance sheet financing. Look at the accounting policies on consolidation and leasing. Look very closely at the note concerning contingent liabilities.

21. See what sort of funds the company has received, apart from profits generated from its operations. How has it used those funds? What are likely future requirements for funds for increased working capital? Consider the company's expansion programme and its capital expenditure programme.

22. Look at your company's audited accounts from the point of view of an outsider, an investor, a supplier, and/or a bank. How would you now react to the figures if you were any of these people?

23. When making comparisons between different companies make sure that the information on each company is really comparable.

Appendix – Infallible Limited Accounts 30 September 1987

Set out below are the accounts of the Infallible group for the year ended 30 September 1987, as sent to shareholders from which the examples in the book are drawn.

Infallible Limited
Report of the Directors

The directors present their report and accounts for the year ended 30 September 1987.

DIRECTORS

The directors who served during the year were:

A T Green
Mrs B White
P L Stevens
W A Brass

W A Brass retires by rotation and, being eligible, offers himself for re-election.

PRINCIPAL ACTIVITY AND BUSINESS REVIEW

The principal activity of the group throughout the year has been the manufacture and distribution of colour designs.

The results for the year and the financial position at the year end were considered satisfactory by the directors who expect continued growth in the foreseeable future.

FIXED ASSETS

Details of changes in the fixed assets are shown in the attached accounts.

In the opinion of the directors the freehold land and buildings has a market value of £50,000 in excess of the amount shown in the accounts.

DIRECTORS' INTERESTS

The directors had the following interests in the shares of the company at the beginning and end of the year:

A T Green	2,000
Mrs B White	2,000
P L Stevens	1,000
W A Brass	500

RESEARCH AND DEVELOPMENT

The group continues its policy of investment in research and development in order to maintain a competitive position in the market.

DONATIONS

The group made charitable contributions during the year amounting to £1,500.

DIVIDENDS

The directors do not recommend the payment of a dividend.

FUTURE DEVELOPMENTS

Approval has been given for the construction of a new factory which is expected to be completed by the summer of 1988; this will increase the group's production capacity by 20%.

AUDITORS

A resolution will be submitted at the annual general meeting proposing that Tried, Tested & Co. be reappointed auditors and that their audit fee for the ensuing year be agreed with the directors.

A T Green
Chairman

31 October 1987

Report of the Auditors to the Members of Infallible Limited

We have audited the accounts on pages 4 to 15 in accordance with approved auditing standards.

In our opinion these accounts give a true and fair view of the state of affairs of the company and the group at 30 September 1987 and of the profit and source and application of funds of the group for the year ended on that date and comply with the Companies Act 1985.

TRIED, TESTED & CO
Chartered Accountants

77 Audit Row,
London EC1

31 October 1987

Infallible Limited
Consolidated Profit and Loss Account
for the Year Ended 30 September 1987

	Note	*1987* £	*1986* £
Turnover	2	3,400,000	3,000,000
Cost of sales		1,200,000	1,150,000
Gross profit		2,200,000	1,850,000
Operating expenses	3	1,810,000	1,665,700
		390,000	184,300
Other income	4	6,400	5,700
		396,400	190,000
Interest payable and similar charges	5	23,400	11,000
Profit on ordinary activities before taxation	6	373,000	179,000
Tax on profit on ordinary activities	7	130,000	66,300
Profit on ordinary activities after taxation		243,000	112,700
Profit attributable to minority interests		1,000	700
Extraordinary item	8	40,000	–
Profit for the financial year		202,000	112,000
Retained profit at 1 October 1986		446,000	334,000
Retained profit at 30 September 1987		648,000	446,000

Infallible Limited
Consolidated Balance Sheet
as at 30 September 1987

		1987		*1986*	
	Note	£	£	£	£
Fixed assets					
Intangible assets	9	7,850		2,700	
Tangible assets	10	166,815		154,020	
			174,665		156,720
Current assets					
Stocks	12	500,000		500,000	
Debtors	13	662,000		485,000	
Investments	14	4,550		4,000	
Cash at bank and in hand		450		5,500	
		1,167,000		994,500	
Creditors – amounts falling due within one year	15	656,106		674,180	
Net current assets			510,894		320,320
Total assets less current liabilities			685,559		477,040
Creditors – amounts falling due after more than one year	16	10,559		6,040	
Provisions for liabilities and charges	17	8,000		7,000	
			18,559		13,040
			667,000		464,000

Financed by:

Capital and reserves			
Called up share capital	18	10,000	10,000
Share premium account		4,000	4,000
Profit and loss account		648,000	446,000
		662,000	460,000
Minority interests		5,000	4,000
		667,000	464,000

A T Green } Directors
P L Stevens }

Approved by the board on
31 October 1987

Infallible Limited
Balance Sheet
as at 30 September 1987

	Note	*1987* £	£	*1986* £	£
Fixed assets					
Intangible assets	9	6,650		900	
Tangible assets	10	166,815		154,020	
Investments	11	39,150		39,150	
			212,615		194,070
Current assets					
Stocks	12	490,000		475,000	
Debtors	13	578,944		438,250	
Investments	14	4,550		4,000	
Cash at bank and in hand		450		5,500	
		1,073,944		922,750	
Creditors – amounts falling due within one year	15	640,500		664,780	
Net current assets			433,444		257,970
Total assets less current liabilities			646,059		452,040
Creditors – amounts falling due after more than one year	16	10,559		6,040	
Provisions for liabilities and charges	17	8,000		7,000	
			18,559		13,040
			627,500		439,000

	Note				
Financed by:					
Capital and reserves					
Called up share capital	18	10,000		10,000	
Share premium account			4,000		4,000
Profit and loss account		613,500		425,000	
		627,500		439,000	

A T Green } Directors
P L Stevens }

Approved by the board on
31 October 1987

Infallible Limited
Statement of Source and Application of Funds
for the Year Ended 30 September 1987

	1987		*1986*	
	£	£	£	£
Source of funds				
Profit before taxation		373,000		179,000
Extraordinary item before tax relief		(57,000)		–
		316,000		179,000
Items not involving the movement of funds:				
Depreciation	21,205		15,200	
Profit on disposal of fixed assets/1986:Loss	(3,150)		2,100	
		18,055		17,300
Funds generated from trading		334,055		196,300
Other sources				
Proceeds from disposal of fixed assets	11,000		10,500	
Proceeds from loans falling due after more than one year	4,519		–	
		15,519		10,500
Total funds generated		349,574		206,800
Application of funds				
Purchase of fixed assets	47,000		24,000	
Tax paid	65,000		103,000	
Dividend paid	–		100,000	
		112,000		227,000
Net inflow of funds/ 1986: Outflow		237,574		(20,200)

Increase/(Decrease) in working capital				
Debtors	177,000		120,000	
Investments	550		–	
Creditors	(63,000)		130,000	
		114,550		250,000
Movement in net liquid funds:				
Cash and bank balances	(5,050)		10,020	
Bank overdraft	128,074		260,180	
		123,024		270,200
		237,574		(20,200)

Infallible Limited
Notes to the Accounts
for the Year Ended 30 September 1987

1. *Accounting Policies*

(a) Accounting convention
The accounts have been prepared under the historical cost convention.

(b) Basis of consolidation
The consolidated accounts include the company and its subsidiaries for the year.

(c) Deferred taxation
Deferred taxation is provided in respect of taxation reliefs which are not expected to continue for the foreseeable future.

(d) Depreciation
Depreciation of fixed assets is provided at the following annual rates by the straight line method:

Freehold land	nil
Freehold buildings	2%
Plant and machinery	20%
Fixtures and equipment	15%
Motor vehicles	25%
Patent and trade marks	10%
Goodwill	20%

(e) Foreign currencies
Assets and liabilities expressed in foreign currencies are translated to sterling at rates of exchange ruling at the end of the financial year. All exchange differences are dealt with in the profit and loss account.

(f) Research and development
Research and development expenditure is written off in the year in which it is incurred.

(g) Stocks
Stocks are stated at the lower of cost and net realisable value. Cost includes all direct costs incurred in bringing the stocks to their present location and condition, including an appropriate proportion of manufacturing overheads.

(h) Turnover
Turnover represents the invoiced value of goods sold, excluding sale between group companies, value added tax and trade discounts.

	1987	*1986*
	£	£
2. *Turnover*		
Geographical analysis:		
United Kingdom	3,000,000	2,700,000
North America	400,000	300,000
	3,4000,000	3,000,000
3. *Operating Expenses*		
Distribution costs	800,000	740,000
Administrative expenses	1,010,000	925,700
	1,810,000	1,665,700
4. *Other income*		
Other operating income	700	–
Income from other investments (Note 4(a))	4,900	5,700
Other interest receivable and similar income	800	–
	6,400	5,700
4(a) *Income from other investments*		
Dividends from listed investments	270	260
Rent receivable	4,630	5,440
	4,900	5,700
5. *Interest payable and similar charges*		
Bank overdrafts	23,000	10,700
Loans repayable within five years	400	300
	23,400	11,000

6. *Profit on ordinary activities before taxation*

After charging:

Auditors' remuneration	6,000	5,500
Depreciation	21,205	15,200
Directors' emoluments (Note 20)	91,000	85,000
Hire of plant and machinery	3,800	1,000

The company has taken advantage of the legal dispensation allowing it not to publish a separate profit and loss account. The profit for the year after tax and extraordinary item attributable to the parent company is £196,000 (1986: £111,000).

7. *Tax on profit on ordinary activities*

Corporation tax based on the results for the year at a rate of 35%	129,000	64,300
Deferred taxation	1,000	2,000
	130,000	66,300

8. *Extraordinary item*

Costs of closure of Pink division	57,000	–
Less: tax relief	17,000	–
	40,000	–

9. *Intangible assets*

Group

	Patent and trade marks	*Goodwill*	*Total*
Cost	£	£	£
At 1 October 1986	1,000	3,000	4,000
Additions	8,000	–	8,000
Disposals	1,500	–	1,500
30 September 1987	7,500	3,000	10,500
Depreciation			
At 1 October 1986	*100*	*1,200*	*1,300*
Charge for the year	*900*	*600*	*1,500*
Disposals	*150*	–	*150*
At 30 September 1987	*850*	*1,800*	*2,650*

Net book value			
At 30 September 1987	6,650	1,200	7,850
At 30 September 1986	900	1,800	2,700

Company

Cost		
At 1 October 1986	1,000	1,000
Additions	8,000	8,000
Disposals	1,500	1,500
At 30 September 1987	7,500	7,500
Depreciation		
At 1 October 1986	100	100
Charge for the year	900	900
Disposals	150	150
At 30 September 1987	850	850
Net book value		
At 30 September 1987	6,650	6,650
At 30 September 1986	900	900

10. *Tangible fixed assets*

Group and company	*Freehold land and buildings*	*Plant and machinery*	*Fixtures and equipment*	*Motor vehicles*	*Total*
Cost	£	£	£	£	£
At 1 October 1986	128,000	37,000	9,000	6,000	180,000
Additions	–	20,000	4,000	15,000	39,000
Disposals	–	5,000	–	6,000	11,000
At 30 September 1987	128,000	52,000	13,000	15,000	208,000
Depreciation					
At 1 October 1986	*9,920*	*11,320*	*3,240*	*1,500*	*25,980*
Charge for the year	*2,480*	*10,736*	*1,614*	*4,875*	*19,705*
Disposals	–	*3,000*	–	*1,500*	*4,500*
At 30 September 1987	*12,400*	*19,056*	*4,854*	*4,875*	*41,185*

Net book value					
At 30 September 1987	115,600	32,944	8,146	10,125	166,815
At 30 September 1986	118,080	25,680	5,760	4,500	154,020

11. *Investments*

Shares in group companies – at cost	39,150	39,150

Name of company and country of incorporation	*Description of shares held*	*Proportion held Direct*	*Indirect*	*Activity*
Bertie Limited (England)	Ordinary shares	100%	–	Manufacture of colour designs
Cecil Limited (Scotland)	Ordinary shares	100%	–	Designers
Dellboy Limited (England)	Ordinary shares	–	75%	Distribution of colour designs

	1987 Group	1987 Company	1986 Group	1986 Company
	£	£	£	£
12. *Stocks*				
Raw materials and consumables	85,000	85,000	100,000	100,000
Work-in-progress	215,000	215,000	175,000	175,000
Finished goods and goods for resale	200,000	190,000	225,000	200,000
	500,000	490,000	500,000	475,000
13. *Debtors – Amounts falling due within one year*				
Trade debtors	579,000	481,944	420,000	362,250
Amounts owed by subsidiary companies	–	17,000	–	12,500
Other debtors	31,000	31,000	25,000	25,000
Prepayments and accrued income	52,000	49,000	40,000	38,500
	662,000	578,944	485,000	438,250

14. *Investments*				
Listed investments – at cost (Market value £7,640/1986:£5,360)	4,550	4,550	4,000	4,000
15. *Creditors – amounts falling due within one year*				
Debenture loans	500	500	500	500
Bank loans and overdrafts	132,106	132,106	260,180	260,180
Trade creditors	347,000	337,224	295,000	290,350
Corporation tax	112,000	112,000	65,000	65,000
Other taxation and social security	33,550	30,500	26,500	24,750
Other creditors	14,450	13,170	12,500	11,500
Accruals and deferred income	16,500	15,000	14,500	12,500
	656,106	640,500	674,180	664,780

The bank loans and overdrafts are secured by a floating charge over the assets of the company.

	1987		*1986*	
	Group	*Company*	*Group*	*Company*
	£	£	£	£
16. *Creditors – amounts falling due after more than one year*				
Debenture loans	3,000	3,000	3,500	3,500
Bank loans and overdrafts due within five years	7,559	7,559	2,540	2,540
	110,559	10,559	6,040	6,040

The debenture loan is repayable in equal annual instalments until 1994. The loan carries interest at 12½% and is secured by a floating charge over the assets of the company.

The bank loan carries interest at 3% over base rate and is secured by a floating charge over the assets of the company.

	1987	1986
	£	£
17. *Provisions for liabilities and charges*		
Group and company		
Deferred taxation		
Accelerated capital allowances	8,000	7,000
18. *Called up share capital*		
Authorised:		
Ordinary shares of £1 each	25,000	25,000
Allotted, called up and fully paid:		
Ordinary shares of £1 each	10,000	10,000
19. *Capital commitments*		
Expenditure contracted but not provided for in the financial statements	12,000	27,000
Approved by the directors but not yet contracted for	200,000	–
20. *Directors' emoluments and higher paid employees*		
Chairman	30,000	28,000
Highest paid director	32,000	39,000

The other directors fall within the following ranges:	*Number*	*Number*
£0 – £ 5,000	–	1
£ 5,001 – £10,000	1	–
£10,001 – £15,000	–	1
£15,001 – £20,000	1	–

21. *Employee information*

The average number of persons employed by the group (including directors) during the year was:

	1987	1986
Production	23	22
Selling and distribution	15	15
Administration	10	9
	48	46

Their total remuneration was:	£	£
Wages and salaries	427,165	392,165
Social security costs	39,603	34,063
Other pension costs	27,416	22,177
	494,184	448,405

Index